THE SUNDAY TIMES

Managing Successful Teams

Pat Wellington

KoganPage

LONDON PHILADELPHIA NEW DELHI

Publisher's note
Every possible effort has been made to ensure that the information contained in this book is accurate at the time of going to press, and the publishers and author cannot accept responsibility for any errors or omissions, however caused. No responsibility for loss or damage occasioned to any person acting, or refraining from action, as a result of the material in this publication can be accepted by the editor, the publisher or the author.

First published in Great Britain and the United States in 2012 by Kogan Page Limited

120 Pentonville Road
London N1 9JN
United Kingdom
www.koganpage.com

1518 Walnut Street, Suite 1100
Philadelphia PA 19102
USA

4737/23 Ansari Road
Daryaganj
New Delhi 110002
India

© Pat Wellington, 2012

ISBN   978 0 7494 6440 0
E-ISBN   978 0 7494 6441 7

The views expressed in this book are those of the author, and are not necessarily the same as those of Times Newspapers Ltd.

British Library Cataloguing-in-Publication Data

A CIP record for this book is available from the British Library.

Library of Congress Cataloging-in-Publication Data

Wellington, Patricia.
  Managing successful teams / Pat Wellington. – 1st ed.
    p. cm.
  Includes bibliographical references.
  ISBN 978-0-7494-6440-0 – ISBN 978-0-7494-6441-7   1. Virtual work teams–Management.   2. Leadership.   3. Computer networks.   I. Title.
  HD66.W445 2012
  658.4'022–dc23

                                                2011047996

Typeset by Graphicraft Ltd, Hong Kong
Printed and bound in India by Replika Press Pvt Ltd

To my dear friend Suzy

Contents

Preface

Let's face it, the business world moves fast. Very fast.

As the forces outside the organisation continue to exert pressures and change, the structures inside organisations need to become more fluid in character so that they respond appropriately. Rather than having people permanently assigned to a particular work team, team composition will shift as projects, problems or customers demand. The result? Your role and responsibilities can change in the blink of an eye.

Just doing the same things and expecting different outcomes is a recipe for disaster. If you think you can stay snuggled up in that same management role for the next few years, forget it. Get ready for the change and the new type of team you are going to be in and must manage. This book is about embracing this challenge, and is written in acknowledgement of the marketplace and the organisation as it is today.

The book is founded on the premise that you have been recruited to join an organisation and take on the management role of a team, or you have been internally promoted into this role. What are some of the work group options you could be joining? What exactly should you do if you are responsible for managing others? How can you adapt to changing circumstances and work and/or manage in a variety of team scenarios and deliver pretty well immediate results?

What's the best type of team structure? A team can be formed in all shapes and sizes. You could be joining a functional team, for example HR or Finance, or be asked to head up a new project, or even a short assignment as part of a task group. Maybe the team does not already exist and you are given the opportunity to recruit from scratch. Or the team might exist already and you are to be its new team leader. A further option could be that you are to lead and manage a remote/virtual team with people you have to work with spread around the world.

Each of these situations will mean you have to adopt different tactics, and consider different ways of managing the team to keep it on track and achieving its objectives. This book will help and guide you through all these different circumstances and give you sensible, *pragmatic* advice for overcoming obstacles you might encounter along the way. My goal ultimately is to help you to create a high performing team that is a joy to lead and work with.

Of course there are similarities in the way that you facilitate and develop your team regardless of what type of group it is, and several chapters will be dedicated to this. Topics such as managing performance, motivation, reward, running projects and tackling issues that might arise during any assignment will all be explored in depth, as will handling people problems, be they members of the team, internal staff, or external stakeholders.

Just think about some of the things that might go through your mind if you have been asked to set up a team from scratch:

- **Starting with the fundamentals – what is it that makes a team a high performing team?**
- **When recruiting people, what mix of skills and competencies will you need for the team to perform well?**
- **Life is not perfect – and even if you have choice of personnel, sometimes one particular person has to play several roles in addition to his or her formal job description. What might these team roles be?**

- How about if you are taking over an existing team? What might be going through your mind? You could be faced with two different situations: the previous manager was fired, or the person previously in the post is now to be your manager.
- How should you manage these two situations? How can you build trust and gain respect with this existing team when 'they have seen all of this before'? And how do you 'politically' handle this, bring in the changes you want, and build a good rapport with the previous manager?
- Supposing you have to take on staff at different stages in their career, for example, one person is a recent graduate and another coasting towards retirement. How best is it to utilise their skills sets and knowledge for the good of the team?
- And finally, suppose you are to take over a virtual team; what might be your thoughts and concerns?
  - How are you going to get this disparate group of people from around the world to feel part of one team?
  - How does your management style need to differ with people working on different continents and in different time zones?
  - How do you successfully manage remotely?
  - How should you go about performance management?

All of these questions, and much more will be answered in this book.

How this book is laid out

The aim of this book is to be a quick, easy guide for readers to dip in and out of as their needs arise. Chapters are stand alone. You don't have to read everything that has come before or after to make sense of the topic in hand. There are hints and tips throughout and current case studies to bring a subject to life and see how companies have put things into action.

I have used the term 'team leader' throughout as a form of shorthand for anyone that has to manage any type of team. Your job title might be this, or manager, project leader, supervisor or facilitator. All the advice is pertinent whatever your job title, as long as you have to manage people in one form of team or another.

How this book is organised

The first three chapters take you through the fundamentals of teamwork, and how to build a new team from scratch.

Chapters 4 and 5 give you robust information on managing the team once formed. In any team you need to be able to motivate, manage performance and reward, and these are covered in Chapter 4. Chapter 5 looks at three other key activities that you will have to undertake in leading a team: setting up communication channels that work, running meetings so that they are effective, and undertaking a project, be it for improvement purposes, new product/service development, etc.

Chapter 6 moves on to a new theme: what are the specific issues and considerations that you might encounter in taking over an existing team? The scenario will be different to setting up a team from scratch.

Inevitably there are going to be problems within the team, and Chapter 7 takes you through a range of issues or problems that you might encounter, and how best to resolve these and build a cohesive team. Managing a virtual team will yet again involve special considerations and this will be looked at in depth in Chapter 8. In the final summary chapter we will look at a projection at how teams might develop in future years.

A team of one is a very lonely place. It doesn't work! In the words of W Edward Deming: 'It's not necessary to change. Survival is not mandatory.'

I welcome hearing about your own experiences managing teams. Do drop me a line at the e-mail address below.

Enjoy the read, and the journey.

Pat Wellington
e-mail: pat@pwellington.plus.com

1

Setting the scene

Introduction

Your working role in life never stands still. You might start working as part of a work group, then become a member of a team and progress to becoming a team leader, possibly in a functional team. As your company grows and expands you could move into a self-managed team, or become a sponsor, or be asked to lead a virtual team. To cut to the chase: you need to develop a broad spectrum of knowledge and understanding, and have all your senses on high alert to develop your various roles, subtly change your style of management and behaviour according to the situation you find yourself in.

But what about the big picture? What is happening in the marketplace and why? How is this going to impact on our working lives?

Big picture

Even before the economic downturn, organisations have been in a state of change and restructuring often to survive, and then to compete on the global platform. This has involved either restructuring, de-layering, or corporate re-engineering, and the introduction of teams. This has allowed organisations to become either more specialised and/or more flexible in order to offer a product or service to the market, to be one step ahead and gain market share.

We have seen how manufacturers are returning to work-group teams, and how electronic communications enable teams to successfully operate even though their members are geographically widely dispersed. Organisations, whether private or public, have woken up to the fact that they do not need to control production in order to supply a service or product, and that in many cases vertical integration is inefficient since specialist providers can satisfy demands for 'components' more cheaply and to higher standards than in-house providers. 'Outsourcing', traditional for the materials and components inputs to many industries, is now becoming common for services and intangible inputs as well as physical components, consumables and sub-assemblies. At the same time, electronic communications have facilitated Just-in-Time manufacturing and inventory techniques, and forced organisations to recognise that one key to competitiveness is long-term and close relationships and teamwork with suppliers. In fact, the supplier is no longer a commercial slave to be whipped but a commercial colleague to be nurtured. Design and manufacturing teams are becoming more and more inter-enterprise, working alongside in-enterprise management teams.

The final step in this process was and is for organisations to 'deconstruct' themselves. Instead of being a monolithic structure, arranged in a pyramid with the chairman at the top and the workers at the bottom, with multiple layers of fossilised management systems in between, the whole edifice is dissolving into small independent work groups, each able to 'sell' some service or value to others. The idea is for teams to come together, involving individuals or groups from around (and outside) the enterprise, perform some activity, be it on a project or long-term production basis, and then dissolve, with the members re-forming into new teams to meet new challenges. Apart from a very small core of strategists and controllers, the 'organisation' in the ordinary sense of the word is on the verge of collapse, to be replaced with something resembling a shoal of fish or flock of migrating birds, splitting, re-forming and wheeling about to avoid dangers and to take advantage of current and short-lived sources of food. With the aid of electronic communications networks, many team members may work wherever they prefer to be, and the 'office' is becoming a pit stop rather than a residence, and 'groupware' is replacing the conference room.

Meanwhile, as the framework dissolves the teams live on, with key individuals perhaps being members of many teams simultaneously, providing personal and information links between them, and ensuring rapid flows of knowledge and 'best practice' from team to team. Teamwork has become the name of the game!

The pros and cons of teamwork

Any research on teams that we have undertaken in organisations has usually given us a positive feedback. Those organisations that have successfully implemented teams have found that communication has improved across the company, and there is a marked improvement in relationships and collaboration between departments, functions or teams. They have also found that they have managed to unlock hidden gems of knowledge and sharing of experiences between those in the teams. There have been 'buy-in' and a sense of ownership demonstrated by those who have undertaken a task or project. Another benefit has been improvements in the way resources are used, resulting in increased effectiveness, efficiency or productivity.

Well stop there. Isn't this too good to be true? Yes, it is. There is a plethora of books and conference presentations talking about 'why teams fail'. So let's look at negative experiences as well, even for those companies that have ultimately successfully implemented teamwork company-wide.

The first stumbling block has been the amount of time it has taken to get teams up and running. Most teams will experience a drop in productivity to start off with while they get established, and this can affect morale. As a result, managers can then panic, as it is still common practice in most organisations in the West to focus on quarterly results. Even when organisations pilot the formation and use of a team there can be resentment from other parts of the workforce, or attempts to sabotage the initiative by senior personnel in the company who have not bought into the concept in the first place. It takes nerves of steel for the steering committee/senior management to stay convinced that implementing teams company-wide is the answer. In many instances it can take from three to five years for work teams to be fully and successfully implemented.

Another major stumbling block has been that the change in the role of managers to whom teams report (as distinct to team leaders) is radical and unexpectedly difficult. Manager as facilitator and manager as coach roles, even when anticipated and sometimes even trained for, often turn out to be deeply unsatisfactory to line managers.

There can also be resentment or 'turf wars' caused by decision-making abilities being transferred from a department to a team. For example, we worked on a customer care initiative with a London borough. One of the issues identified during the assignment was the fact that the one-stop call centre that had been created to offer a range of primary services had real difficulties initially getting even basic information. Individual departments would simply not provide information for the call centre to do its work properly. Staff in these departments saw the call centre as 'new upstarts', who might have good communication skills but could not possibly have the knowledge or intelligence to handle even basic, non-essential queries that related to the services they traditionally offered.

In reality many of the fundamental enquiries that people in these departments handled were an irritation and interrupted them undertaking the core parts of their workload. But at the same time they were clearly concerned as to how centralised the information or services from their department were going to be made, and the impact on their jobs. The approach often was, 'If you don't know what is going to happen it is better to resist.'

On balance, in spite of these negative experiences, I believe teamworking often provides an organisational effectiveness that usually exceeds that which is achieved by a traditional hierarchical chain of command. The flexibility and agility that are enabled by teams means companies can come to market with a new product or service not only to keep abreast of market trends but also to beat the competition. In addition, the emphasis on more people-centred companies where employees have the benefit of formal systems for their appraisal, the analysis of their training needs and assessment of the results achieved both personally and by the team, have all been part and parcel of how this has been achieved.

As we start to move through the book you will see that there is a considerable investment to be made – in planning, managerial time, training and opportunity cost to create a high performing team. The setting up of a team or teams within an organisation cannot happen without support from the top.

What support do teams need from the top?

How successful an organisation is at utilising teamwork effectively largely depends on the attitude, directives and policies that come from the management team. So what's of importance?

- **Too much hierarchy whether formal or informal can impede teamwork.**
- **Resources need to be sufficient for a team to function. This means right staffing levels, budget, equipment, and a way of accessing up-to-the-minute information.**
- **Encouragement of teams to work collaboratively rather than in competition with each other. It is important that these work groups set their goals in harmony**

with each other and that the goals are mutually
supportive.
- Reward systems that recognise team performance
  as well as individual contributions.
- Teams need to have the authority to act upon their
  teams' decisions.

Bearing all of this in mind, where do we go from here? For starters
you need to understand the difference between a team and a work
group and the various types of teams that might be developed
within a company. So over and out to the next chapter.

2

Back to basics – the fundamentals of working in teams

Introduction

So we need to start from the basics. First, are teams always the answer? Do you really work in a team, or some other form of group? What is the definition of a team? Are there different types of teams and, if so, what are they? What are the considerations in structuring a team? What stages might a team go through in its development? What are the two critical roles that can make a difference between success and failure? What are the characteristics of a high performing team?

What is and what isn't a team?

The creation of a team is not the answer in every situation that might arise within a company. If, for example, a group's work is

routine and unchallenging and wholly pre-programmed with no
opportunity for feedback, developing a team will not make much
difference to productivity.

In a food production line, if you take a bunch of staff doing
a manual activity, for example, ensuring the washed lettuce leaves
are evenly spread out across a conveyor belt or putting the stuffing
in turkeys, there is little point in putting them in yellow jump
suits and calling them the 'leaf squad', or 'turkey finishers squad',
and telling them to self-manage. It is unlikely to pay off with
them making more effort or using more common sense or brain
power than they would normally do. The group would see this as
'another management fad', and get on with their work as usual.

When a group of people work together it does not necessarily
mean that they are working as a team. If you find yourself working
with others to share perspective or information, rather than to
create a specific goal, you are working as part of a group. Groups
don't expect their individual contribution to *create added value*
to the whole.

There are also task groups in organisations. The task itself
can usually provide the initial motivation to work together, but
to make working together a success more is needed. A team is
not just a group of individuals working in isolation. Planning
and scheduling of activities is a given first step, plus dealing
with factual content. This is not enough in its own right.
People need to relate socially and have a feeling of trust and
interest in each other; it is not just about process-oriented
aspects of work.

Teams, on the other hand, especially those with increased
autonomy and responsibility, are more effective when their
members are given complex tasks that capitalise on the
diverse knowledge and skills in the team. This is a major
difference to groups. They also perform well when there is
high task interdependence, or a high degree of coordination
and collaboration required to accomplish a variety of tasks.

The effectiveness of teams depends on whether an
organisation has high integrating needs due to operating in
a complex environment. Complex environments typically force

organisations to serve a wide variety of customers, deal with rapidly changing technology, and satisfy large numbers of different stakeholders. Unisys or IBM, for example, face a much more complex environment than McDonald's. Think of the rate of change of PCs and software verses Big Macs over the last 10 years.

'Team' defined

In the current business world you will often meet managers who will talk about their 'team', when in reality they are dealing with a group of individuals whose commonality of purpose is simply to prevent themselves being overwhelmed by the workload.

Jon Katzenbach, Director at McKinsey & Co, and Douglas Smith, have been very influential in the study of teams. In their book *The Wisdom of Teams*, they define teams as follows:

- **Working towards a common goal.**
- **The personal success of team members is dependent on others.**
- **Have an agreed and common approach.**
- **The knowledge and skills of team members are complementary.**
- **A small number of people, usually less than 20.**

As Harvery Robbins and Michael Finley wrote in *Why Teams Don't Work*, a team is about *people doing something together*. It could be a football team playing in a game against opposition, or a research team developing a new pharmaceutical drug, or a rescue team pulling people out from a burning building. The *something* that a team does isn't what makes it a team; the *together* part is.

Teams can be constituted in a variety of ways, as shown in Table 2.1, including working remotely in a virtual team. These are developed for a variety of reasons:

- new product or service development;
- company start-ups;
- home-based work and teleworking;
- distribution purposes.

As mentioned above, team membership might be relatively stable, for example an established sales team, or change on a regular basis as happens in project teams.

Table 2.1   The different make-up of teams

From	To
Fixed team membership	Shifting team membership
People are part of just one team	People are part of multiple teams
Members of the team are all from the same company	Teams are made up of internal staff and people from outside the organisation (eg, suppliers/clients)
The team is located in one location	The team is geographically dispersed
Teams have a fixed start and end date	Teams form and re-form on a regular basis
Teams are managed by one single manager	Teams have multiple reporting arrangements with different parts of the organisation at different times

Different types of teams

The types of teams you will find in an organisation include:

- *Operational* – teams you form part of by joining an organisation, such as HR, Finance, Marketing, etc.

- *Strategic* – this team is focused on providing the organisation or unit with long-term competitive advantage, clear differential in the eyes of its customers. It is dealing with future focus and a host of complex variables.
- *Quality circles* – teams throughout the organisation examining continuous improvement activities.
- *Self-managed teams* – working together in their own way towards a common goal that is *defined outside the team*. For example, on a production line, the senior management will have decided on the packaging/cardboard boxes to be used for containing a product, but the team will do their own work scheduling/training/creating rewards and recognition.
- *Self-directed teams* – as above, working towards a common goal that *the team defines*, but also handling compensation, discipline and acting as a profit centre by defining its own future. For example, in a university a commercial unit could be set up to handle in-house assignments with corporate clients, and be reliant on generating sufficient income to cover its own costs and generate profit.

Groups formed for a limited period and for a clearly defined set of circumstances include:

- *Task force/project teams* – set up for problem-solving activities. This type of team will often be staffed by members of the organisation who have clout, and therefore be in a position of authority and able to implement the recommended changes that are required for problems to be resolved. Project teams are also set up for new product development, and the creation of new services.
- *Cross-functional teams* – these are normally set up for a limited time in which to complete a sensitive task such as new product development, or improvement to a

process. They could be staffed, for example, by people from Finance/Marketing/HR and Operations, and also could include a supplier or client. They need to draw on information from all parts of the business, including information from functional departments. System integration becomes important because it makes all information accessible through a single interface. They might need three types of information to be used for strategic/tactical and operational decisions, as required for new product development. Cross-functional teams could also make decisions on inventory purchase/ production scheduling and whether to test-market a product or service.

It is important that teams are designed around the tasks they perform. A team should be relatively self-contained and should handle many aspects of its own functioning, including support services, so that it has the resources necessary to accomplish its goals. They should be able to apply the team's resources, the strategies for completion of work, and monitoring quality. They should be responsible for working with internal and external customers. Part of the team's task should include performance evaluation. Members should be multi-skilled and dedicated to the team so that they do not have to split priorities. The team should report as a unit so that they don't have conflicting directions from different managers.

CASE STUDY   Boeing

At Long Beach, California, Boeing manufactured the 717 plane, a 100-seat short range aircraft designed for the commuter market.

In 1996 orders were low, and the project was losing money. Management decided they needed to either call it a day and stop manufacturing the aircraft, or find major efficiencies to bring in the production of the aircraft profitably. They decided to take the second option. By 2000 Boeing had outperformed the competition, selling 19 of its aircraft. Airbus Industries, one of its rivals, sold only three of its comparable sized A318. It had also managed to reduce the manufacturing time of the plane from six to four days.

How did it achieve this turnaround in its fortunes? Boeing decided to focus on three areas:

1. Implementing a team-based structure.
2. Improving the training of staff.
3. Introducing lean manufacturing techniques.

Self-managed teams were created, grouping staff according to their functions, not their titles. For example, instead of housing all the engineers in a separate building they grouped them in teams around a specific task. Members of all functions – from finance and labour unions to engineering and product support, were also grouped together around specific tasks such as interior design, final assembly, propulsion and product delivery.

Improved training involved staff learning about labour-saving techniques, and becoming financial aware (internal return on investment and shareholder value). Lean manufacturing taught them how to improve workflow and cut costs. For instance, more than 5 million square feet of space at the facility were sold and personnel working on the 717 aircraft were moved to a single space – a 600,000 square foot factory.

The workflow process was then redesigned so teams worked side by side on a full moving production line, a first for a commercial plane. For example, the person who designs the seat is next to the person who builds them. Support teams are located within a few feet of the assembly positions. They are equipped with everything they need to keep the planes moving, including specialists who inspect work while it is being done.

(Based on Gale, 2000, pp 60–67)

Stages of team development

In 1965 Barry Tuckman described four main stages of group development which have been verified by research. He explained that groups must experience various developmental stages before they become fully productive and functioning as a group entity. Some groups become stuck in a particular phase of growth for varying lengths of time, thus moving through the phases of growth is unique to each individual group and learning happens at each stage. As Yalom (1970) says, 'a freely interactive group... will, in time, develop into a social microcosm of the participant members'.

However, for optimum group performance all four stages need to be negotiated. These stages are Forming, Storming, Norming and Performing. In the counselling and psychotherapy world, the fifth stage – Mourning – is vital.

When a group of people are put together to form a team, they don't necessarily know each other. There is unfamiliarity, and time and energy are spent assessing each other and jockeying for position. The focus on purpose and objectives, what the team is set up to achieve, becomes secondary to these necessary preliminaries.

Forming (coming together)

This is like the first week on a training course – a gathering of disparate individuals, trying to find out about each other. At this stage individuals are trying to assess attitudes, background of other members, and establishing their own persona in the group. Some members will test the tolerance of both systems and the leader. On the whole, most members of the group are on their 'best behaviour' at this time.

Individual roles and responsibilities will be unclear, and there will be a high dependence on the team leader for guidance and direction.

Storming (open conflict)

The group will have now come together and individuals start to sort out and negotiate what they want out of the group process (whatever the purpose of the group – learning or experiential). This is often a very uncomfortable period. Individual goals are stated and interpersonal clashes result when differences emerge between the goals/needs and wants of individuals. Alliances may be formed, sometimes even subgroups, and initial relationships can be disrupted. The main characteristic is conflict between group members. This is usually regarded as the essential stage of a truly representative group, as it is, of course, a democratic process. Without the support of the team leader in negotiating this tricky stage, groups can remain secretly divided and less functional/creative.

If these differences are not negotiated or aired, individuals operate within their own hidden agenda and hinder the healthy functioning of the group.

Norming (settling)

Agreement and consensus is largely formed amongst the team, and roles and responsibilities established. The 'rules' and 'norms' of the group have been accepted; for example no talking or interrupting while another team member is speaking during a meeting, how open communication is to be amongst the team, or practical considerations such as lunchtime cover.

The team leader will delegate smaller decisions to individuals or a few people within the group.

Performing (executing task)

At this stage the team are more strategically aware – they know clearly why they are doing what they are doing. This is the stage that the group is functioning as a team. They are keen to get on with the task and work set. Members take the initiative, cooperate and work interactively to meet stated and shared objectives.

As the team now have a good deal of autonomy, they can make decisions based on criteria established by the team leader. Obviously disagreements will still occur, but now they are resolved within the team. The team does not need to be instructed or assisted, and will come to the team leader occasionally for advice and guidance. This will put the team leader in a position to move on to key activities, and take a more strategic role.

Mourning (letting go)

If a team is ultimately going to disband, this will be at the finish of the task or project. Those people involved will no longer be meeting/functioning as a group entity with a common objective. Relationships between individuals may continue but this particular set-up will be ending. This is often characterised by the stages of grief (which are not sequential – shock, denial, anger, bargaining, letting go/coming to terms with moving on, forever changed by the group experience and its loss).

A team will often believe they are at the Performing stage, when in reality they haven't moved out of the Forming stage. For a team to become a high performing team, they must go through all of these stages in the right order.

Timing of progress through these stages will obviously depend on the nature of the team you are involved with. A functional team that has been together for years will usually take longer to go through these stages, and will almost certainly move backwards and forwards a few times as people leave the team and new arrivals have an impact on the group dynamic. Project teams on the other hand, who are just together for a short period of time, say six months, will have to develop and go through these stages at a quicker pace to be truly effective. Teams of any nature can easily get stuck at one stage, say the Storming stage, if for example roles and responsibilities do not appear to be fairly distributed, or the team cannot agree a common goal or way forward.

Structuring the team

How does the structure of the team have an impact on its effectiveness? Questions to ask are:

- **Is it the right size? Ideally there should be around seven or eight in the team. More than that can make it too challenging to manage.**
- **Have members of the team been able to input their ideas during the design stage of the team?**
- **Does the structure build on the strengths of high performers sufficiently to compensate for any poor performers who it might be obligatory to keep in the team?**
- **Are certain people in the team overstretched by being in two or even three teams concurrently?**
- **Will the duration of the team allow people to bond and feel part of the team?**
- **Does the structure encourage people in the team to link with others whom they normally wouldn't be in contact with of their own accord, but might be needed for advice or supplies during the project?**
- **Should end users, customers, or business representatives be involved from the word go, or once formative ideas have been thought through?**
- **Does the design support a clear understanding of accountability based on shared ownership and collective success?**

CASE STUDY   Typical structure of a software
development project team

Let's take an example of a software development project team.
The various roles in the team will have been identified as part of the
planning, estimating and resourcing process. Inevitably the resources
and the way people work together will change during the project.
Often an initial high powered team will define the business solution,
followed by a much broader team to deliver it, and then a line
management and operational team to operate it. There will be a core
team fully involved throughout the project, but others will be brought
in as required. Team structures will probably be adjusted at each
stage to meet the evolving nature of the project. The right structure
for a small high powered business design team is unlikely to work for
a large application development team.

The typical strategy is to organise a larger team into a collection
of smaller teams. Each sub-team would be responsible for one or more
subsystems, enabling them to work as a small agile team responsible
for delivering working software on a timely basis.

There will be a plethora of other staff involved including a project
sponsor/project director/steering committee/project manager/team
leaders and a coach/coordinator known as a Scrum Master. There will
also be finance and marketing teams which will deliver accounting
and promotional activities.

(Hazrati, 2010)

We work a lot in the world of technology, helping teams to get
back on track, and the consistent theme we hear is that the people
who take 'leadership' or 'management' roles aren't necessarily
the people best placed to do these roles. It could be that they were
recruited into the Scrum Master or leader role because they were
the best technologist, or forcefully opinionated about 'how things
must be'. This is not what is needed. First and foremost you need

someone who is people-oriented, who has people skills and can act as a coach to those in his or her team. This involves listening and encouraging others to come to their own conclusions, not being a 'font of all knowledge' giving instructions to the troops.

This leads us on to exploring two critical roles that define the success or otherwise of a team: the leader and the sponsor.

Two critical roles

There are two leadership roles which are absolutely critical in successful team applications. The first, unsurprisingly, is the *internal team leader*, the person who for want of a better word 'chairs' the team, runs the meetings, supervises the team's processes, and works within the team on a day-to-day basis.

The second is as important: it's the person outside the team to whom it is usually responsible for its activities. Sometimes this person is called the *team's sponsor*. I like the US analogy: it is the person who 'rides shotgun for the team'. In the days of the Wild West, stagecoaches carried a person whose continuous responsibility was to scan the horizon for menacing situations – hostile Indians, robbers or whatever. This person, armed of course – presumably with a shotgun – was also expected to deal with these incidents. He (while I am no expert, I assume there were few, if any women so engaged) had no responsibility other than to ensure the stagecoach operated smoothly, did not run in to trouble, was defended against attacks and so on. It has been my experience that this 'shotgun role' is crucial in setting up and operating successful teams.

Let's look at these leadership roles in more detail.

The team leader

It is important to be clear about the differences between the tasks or responsibilities of the leader, and the qualities or competencies he or she will have to be able to deploy for the team to succeed.

If we look first at the tasks, this might provide us with a useful generic summary:

- **To ensure that the team is 'on-purpose': that it is doing what it is supposed to be doing, that it is on course to achieve the reasons for its creation.**
- **To allocate work and resources within the team.**
- **To make sure that all important team processes take place – the way members interact with each other; the way decisions are taken, the way participation is encouraged, etc.**
- **To ensure the flow of information into, out of, and within the team is operating well.**
- **To manage the time of the team effectively.**

Ultimately the team leader is there to facilitate the team in achieving its results or objectives. More often than not the role involves framing and agreeing those objectives in the first place.

The role of team leader can vary substantially according to the nature of the team that is formed. In certain instances the role is static, but if a team is created that ultimately becomes self-managed, the key roles and responsibilities of the initial team leader can change and develop. So let's look at how this might happen, and the time frame involved.

From team leader to self-managed team

Step 1: 0–9 months
The team is centred on a team leader, who assumes leadership of all team activities, may consult individual team members before making decisions, and is responsible for informing team members.

Step 2: 6–18 months

Decisions are made in consultation with the whole team, as opposed to individually. The team leader is still in a leadership role at all times.

Step 3: 12–30 months

Some team members take on a leadership role for specific issues/activities. The team leader assumes the role of coach to these individuals, and also contributes during discussions.

Step 4: 18–42 months

More team members may step up to take on the leadership role where they have the specialist knowledge or desire to learn.

Step 5: 24 months +

All team members are able to take on a leadership role for specific functions. Cross-training may occur. The team leader now performs business management functions, and acts mainly as a catalyst and influencer for the team when needed.

The sponsor (shotgun rider's) role

If a team is to be successful the sponsor must be very successful in two major areas. The first is the preparatory work in setting up the team:

- **Deciding how, where and what sort of team to put in position.**
- **Recruiting/appointing the members and the team leader.**
- **Setting up the team with a clear mandate, purpose, scope and operating boundaries.**
- **Preparing, informing and reassuring the organisation.**

Once the team is set up, the role switches to creating and managing the right environment in which the team will operate. It involves:

- **procuring resources for the team;**
- **representing the team and their interests to the rest of the organisation;**
- **guarding the team from outside attack by others in the organisation;**
- **acting as facilitator, mentor, counsellor, 'go for', ambassador, adviser, feather smoother, mediator and friend to the team.**

Qualities and competencies of the sponsor

In the early days of the team's establishment and during its formative period, the team is usually highly reliant on its sponsor and dependent on the support, nurturing, counselling and cajoling he or she provides. The critical need is to help the team understand its purpose in being set up. This might sound naively obvious, but it has been my experience that the sponsor frequently spends more time explaining *what* is expected of the team than *why* it is there. The sponsor's role is to make the connection between the organisation's strategic intent and the reason for the team's existence.

Let's take the example of an operational team formed to improve processes and, say, to cut costs. This may sound like a perfectly clear mandate, but it is not. It describes a set of outcomes, not a contribution to the organisation's strategic intent. Cutting costs may be a required outcome because:

- **The organisation is uncompetitive and will reflect the savings of cost cuts in its pricing to a customer.**
- **The organisation is not making sufficient return for its shareholders, in which case the benefit will be reflected in dividends.**
- **The organisation needs to improve its cash flow, in which case improving margins will contribute to more positive cash flows.**

The issue here is that the team's behaviour might be very different depending on what lies behind the cost-cutting objective. Its order of priorities, the objectives it devises for itself and the focus of its energy will all be different depending on the strategic initiatives it is there to support.

It is the sponsor's role to make that link between objectives and organisational strategy and to assert it continuously, unambiguously and honestly. The sponsor must be able to help the team build its vision of what success might look and feel like quantitatively and qualitatively. Evidence is that leaders who build such a vision with their teams are more effective, their teams better grounded and the results more imaginative.

Above all the sponsor must resist the idea of 'selling' the team; the skill is to facilitate the team's buying process. This refers to the 'push/pull' theory of leadership. This theory can be seen in competitive rowing. The leader can row the boat but the paradox of leadership states that the fastest boats were manned by crews that pull together. When you 'facilitate your team's buying process' you allow your employees to pull the 'team boat'. This means that you allow your team to lead itself and allow your team to make mistakes and learn from them through daily, weekly and monthly huddles. Throughout this process, you must stay patient. This is a real challenge for many, especially during turbulent times. By spending more time listening and less time telling the team what to do, you can revitalise teams and entire organisations. In other words, a model for the sponsor during this forming period might look like Table 2.2.

Letting go

Like being a parent, the sponsor of a team that moves towards high performance must learn the skill of progressively letting go. As we can see from above, the role change requires moving from involvement, active facilitation and development, to managing the environment in which the team operates.

Many sponsors find that undertaking this change is surprisingly difficult and case histories are riddled with stories of how sponsors,

Table 2.2   The role of the sponsor during the 'forming' period

Team's need during the forming period	Supporting sponsor/shotgun-rider competence
Establish purpose	To think, talk and present organisational strategy Project honesty and conviction Debate, help unpack, tumble, clarify, explore, explain the team's purpose and its relationship to strategy
Establish a vision of success	Realise it must be the team's vision Help facilitate the team's 'dream': imagine, prompt, applaud, reinforce, clarify, question, help crystallise; insert, if necessary, pragmatism and realism
Establish objectives	Realise they must be the team's objectives Help them develop their objectives (these are often more demanding than any that the sponsor might lay upon them) Help them define the measures – how will we know? Again, pragmatism and realism

accustomed to a high degree of executive control and decision making, feel ignored and left out when the team they have created develops the assurance to take decisions for itself. A feeling of being redundant is widely experienced. Sometimes, rather than basking in the success of the team, sponsors feel a sense of resentment at the ingratitude of the team. Here are some quotes from sponsors finding difficulty with a different role:

> I felt I was placed outside the perimeter fence and was peeking in to see what they were up to at any time.

> I'm really indignant about what they are suggesting... I feel they are usurping my role... I am going to slap them back.

I used to be a hunter. Now I am a farmer.

I feel like Dr Frankenstein – look at the monster I have created!

Taking on this new hands-off role and working to manage the environment is a precondition for the successful operation of the team though, together with careful monitoring of its vital signs. Most sponsors find, however, that the team sometimes hits trouble and needs intervention, redirection or therapy, and they become involved and integrated into the team once more.

Why do teams sometimes not work?

Probably at some point in your career you have worked in a team that simply does not work, for a variety of reasons. It could be structural – how the team has been set up or a lack of clarity about what people should be doing. There could be competiveness within the team, and people keeping back data or information for their own benefit. Sometimes people have to work a 15-hour day to get things done because milestones were not laid out clearly enough to start off with. This can all be down to poor leadership of the team and the way the team has been set up in the first place. As this is a real 'biggy', we are going to look at this thorny topic in more detail in Chapter 7.

The stumbling blocks that can affect the success of the team

There are three basic sets of values that can impact on the success or otherwise of the team:

1. The quality of communication – how people share information, and their willingness to understand the other person's point of view.

2. Is there a common team goal? Is it shared?
3. Respect and trust – are people honest about their needs and requirements? Is there genuine openness and candour? Do those in the team show consideration for each other? Is trust reciprocated?

In most of our everyday life we are primarily judged on our individual performance and actions. When you put people together in a team it does not mean that everyone is going to bond together in 'happy-clappy land'. People can do things consciously or unconsciously that can impact on the effectiveness of the team. Likewise, circumstances outside your team can have an impact. So if it is your responsibility to keep the team on track, you need to have all your antennae on high alert for sussing out the barriers that there might be to your team succeeding. Some of those barriers might be as follows:

- The organisation or senior personnel other than your sponsor do not really support the goals of the team.
- The goals themselves are not implemented.
- There is no real understanding of the mission of the team.
- The mission of the team changes, and all members of the team do not agree with the changes.
- Team members are not prepared to do the work necessary to implement team objectives.
- There are no clearly defined roles established for team members.
- People make commitments that they don't keep.
- There is poor communication with other departments/ teams, internal customers.
- There is poor communication and conflict within the team itself.
- People are very stuck in their ways, and do not want to experiment or try new ways of tackling an assignment.
- Team members practise passive resistance.
- There are no checkpoints established to monitor team behaviour.

Exercise: Barriers to our team's success

Go through the list of barriers above and define what you believe is inhibiting the success of your team. Assess what needs to happen to improve the situation, and draw up a specific timed action plan to take things forward.

The characteristics of a well-functioning team

The way a team plays as a whole determines its success. You may have the greatest bunch of individual stars in the world, but if they don't play together, the club won't be worth a dime. (Babe Ruth)

When a team is performing well there is a definite buzz and feeling of energy and commitment in the air. People in the team understand their roles. There is no job overlap. Goals have been set, which are often challenging. Some drama, urgency and a little fear can be a great boost to drive. With the goals being very specific and timed, everyone knows where they are and what they have to achieve in what time frame. Of course there also needs to be a sense of purpose. Both of these are interdependent. The purpose keeps the long term alive, and the goals the short-term purpose. But what comes first?

Usually a team with a specific goal will find it develops into an overall purpose, for example, reducing production cost by 10 per cent, which may lead to a decision to develop a bigger market share. This is where getting together as a team is vital. Discussions will focus on whether the goal is still appropriate. What are the long-term impacts for the whole business – for the team?

This means communication is key not just between those in the team but with other stakeholders they link with. Communication stretches to how well the team handles interpersonal conflict. Do people always expect the manager to handle these issues or can they sort things out between themselves? This would indicate the maturity of the team.

When projects are set, a high performing team will have a sense of ownership and bring in the project on time and within budget. This can't consistently be the case of course, but high performing teams know what to do when things go wrong, and contingency plans are in place.

This just gives you a bird's eye view of how a high performing team achieves outcomes and moves out of the realm of just simply 'performing'. All of the detail and exploration of different circumstances will follow in the rest of book. In the meantime here is a checklist exercise for you to go through so that you can start to analyse what is or isn't working in your current team.

Exercise: Creating a high performance team

Go through the list below and honestly question and assess how your team stacks up.

1. The organisational environment
- Are things outside the team helping or hindering performance?
- Does the team have adequate resources (people and financial)?
- What about policies, strategies, structures, the market?
- Is the team's mandate understood and widely accepted in the organisation?

2. Goals
- Do people understand and accept the team's primary task (its organisational mandate)?

- Are team members involved in setting objectives?
- Do all individuals agree with the priorities?
- Is progress towards team goals regularly reviewed by the team?

3. Roles
- What do team members expect of one another?
- Are these expectations clear? Acceptable?
- How are conflicts in expectations handled?
- Is unnecessary duplication avoided?
- Who does what?
- Do team members know how their personal efforts contribute to the team's success?

4. Processes
- How are information flow and the need for coordination handled?
- Are all the team members coping with the current technologies?
- How are problems solved, decisions made and adhered to?
- Are meetings efficient and improvement-oriented?
- Are deadlines and milestones clearly established and agreed to by the team?
- Are reporting procedures clear and concise?

5. Relationships
- How do members treat and feel about each other?
- Are peoples' needs for recognition, support and respect adequately met?
- Is there effective analysis and feedback of group and individual performance?
- Are there good communication channels established with other teams and other parts of the organisation?

Checklist for action

- Think about your current situation – are you in a work group or team?
- If you lead a team, are there any structural issues that need to be corrected? If so, take action.
- Put some meat on the bone. Look outside your own team and think what other type of teams, if any, are operating in your company.
- Go through the exercise immediately above looking at the environment, goals, roles, processes and relationships. Define where you and your current team shine, and where there is room for improvement.

3

Setting up a new team

Introduction

So you are the team leader. It's been announced that you are to take up your responsibilities immediately. Your new office is waiting. What happens now? Do you need to recruit your team members from scratch or is there an existing group of individuals, from disparate groups from within the organisation, who you must now mould into a new team?

What is the sequence you should adopt? You must first:

- **Define a concrete, measurable and verifiable objective(s) for the team. I use the term 'concrete' a good deal throughout the book. It means 'what exactly and by when and contains a figure'.**
- **Define the team's job description (responsibilities, skills and personal attributes required). Complete the team job description and then make a list of the skills needed to realise the concrete objectives.**
- **If you can select the team, recruit the best people with these skills. If you are given a group that you must form**

into a team, you need to become aware of individual
limitations and address these as best you can (given
the resources you have to hand).

A 12-step guide for setting up a new team

1. Profile team members

A person's functional role in a team means that he or she supplies
the required technical skills and operational knowledge. You need
more than this for a team to work effectively. There is a secondary
role that people play in a team, consciously or inadvertently, that
can contribute to the overall effectiveness of the team.

Check if your organisation has its own tools to analyse and
know your team members' behavioural preferences. If not, try
using a team-building tool developed by Meredith Belbin, or
Myers-Briggs Type Indicator (MBTI) assessment. Belbin describes
nine team roles that ideally should be present for a team to succeed.
We are going to look at this in more detail later in the chapter as
I think it is an interesting approach to be aware of when you are
creating your team, or needing to recruit and get the balance right
should someone leave.

The Myers-Briggs MBTI tool has been around in theory or
practice since the 1920s. It is a psychometric questionnaire
designed to measure psychological preferences in how people
perceive the world and make decisions. It doesn't reflect a person's
intelligence levels or likelihood of success, but focuses on how
they feel about things: whether they're more practical, whether
they are more emotional, etc. It is obviously important for
motivation purposes that you understand how those in your team
tick. Why do they like doing certain things? What environment
do they work in best? It's also helpful to the team members to
gain more self-knowledge in why they do what they do, why they're
comfortable in certain situations, and uncomfortable in others.

2. Confront reality

Your first priority in creating the team is to orchestrate a carefully coordinated group effort and mobilise them with a view to achieving high performance. You must concentrate on engineering the individual efforts of the team into a unified, coherent, collective effort. You will have to create a team culture and team language relevant to the job in hand. The reality is that your reputation is at stake. The best way to protect that reputation is to get results.

Confronting reality means taking charge. Don't act tentatively in the early stages of constructing your team. Take charge and make things happen. Your effectiveness depends heavily on your credibility with your team members, and you undermine that credibility when you wallow or waffle. People will not rally behind a manager they can't respect. Don't confuse respect with popularity. Focus on getting results.

3. Get 'buy-in'

You need to show members of the team what direction the team is heading in, and also get them to buy in to this direction. Specifically you need to show them:

- **your vision for the future;**
- **a strategy for getting there;**
- **why this is the best strategy;**
- **how every achievement big or small indicates that the team is winning;**
- **the culture of the team.**

Your vision must not only paint a picture, but excite the team with large, desired outcomes. In this context there need to be goals that contain challenges, appeal to personal pride and provide an opportunity to make a difference and know that you are doing so. Buy-in happens when you describe what team success might look like. The sorts of questions you need to be able to answer:

- So what is the end result?
- What should we be aiming for?
- What will it feel like?
- How will others know?
- What must we all do to be successful?

If you address the latter point successfully and explain to your team what you expect from them in the way they work and what they can expect from you in return, it will help to clarify the team's attitude to working together.

4. Be a catalyst, not only a controller

As is a common mantra throughout this book, your role as a leader is to catalyse consensus, not issue orders. Consensus means gathering everyone's thoughts and ideas by asking non-assumptive questions, being a good listener, opening up the discussion to get further input and, finally, getting an agreed decision from the group as to the approach/way forward. You are more likely to get a consensus outcome if people in the team feel their ideas are heard and considered, even though the team as a whole ultimately does not choose those particular ideas.

Know your people (there is more on this later in the chapter). Remember when you are recruiting people to the team that skills can be taught – attitude can't. Sometimes you don't have the luxury of being able to choose who joins the team. Look for strengths and weaker points; aspirations and work preferences; experience and areas of expertise; concerns and points of resistance. The sharper your insights into each individual, the better the odds that you'll manage him or her effectively. Check for people's adaptability. Ask yourself who is best suited for which role.

If there are weak players that you must use position them where they'll hurt the team least. No matter how good you are as a leader, there could be occasions when someone in the team does not pull his or her weight and is proving to have a negative impact on the team's morale. If this is the case you cannot allow that person to compromise your goals and drag the team down with them. Don't be afraid to cut dead wood and find someone who fits your team dynamic and does his or her fair share.

Your key people can be the cornerstones of your team effort, so don't take these people for granted. Make *everyone* feel important. Invest the same time and effort in creating the team that you would in recruiting a new employee. Try to capture people's spirit. Put some fire into their feeling about the work in hand. Ensure they're on board *emotionally*. Successful teamwork depends heavily on your ability to stabilise the group. Do your best to keep it intact.

5. Define roles and responsibilities

Ensure everyone knows what's expected of them. Don't leave people to figure things out on their own. Get rid of rule ambiguity. Nail down every team member's responsibilities with clarity, precision and attention to detail.

There must be no question about where one job stops and the next one starts. Leave no blur regarding the responsibilities each team member is supposed to shoulder. Figure out precisely what needs to be done, who's going to do which part of it, and communicate your plan. Give every team member a brief job description. State your expectations regarding standards of performance. Describe the chain of command in the team. Outline each person's spending limits, decision-making authority and reporting requirements. Everyone will be best served if you put down this information in writing.

Check to make sure that each team member understands the team's (whole) set-up and how it fits together. Be careful to avoid job overlap, since that feeds power struggles, wastes resources and frustrates everyone involved. When explaining to people what to do, also specify what they should *not* do. Differentiate between crucial tasks and peripheral, low priority activities. Spell out what needs to be accomplished in each position and what the person will be held most accountable for. Once you have done this, pay attention to what team members are doing. Keep everyone on track. If you see something going wrong, fix it immediately.

6. Provide tools and processes; remove inhibitors and blockages

While developing your team there are inevitably going to be things that get in the way. Remove inhibitors and blockages. These are typically a lack of resources, information, and processes that people need for their work. It's your job to help remove these obstacles. It could be that equipment is not up to scratch, for example PCs need upgrading, part of the equipment on the production line needs replacing, or there needs to be a telephone to hand in the packaging department for calling suppliers on a Just-in-Time basis.

There could also be people inhibitors – internal colleagues or departments that your team links with regularly who prove to be challenging to deal with (a classic can be a sales team linking with the finance department!) Set up meetings with these internal customers to resolve any conflict or issues between both parties.

Do bear in mind that if you are going to ask people to be creative and push the boundaries, they have to have the appropriate advice, coaching, or training that they may need to do this.

Pay attention to process. Think of this as your team's gearbox, the internal machinery of how it goes about its business. Teams, in principle, should be self-monitoring or self-correcting.

During times of change or transition, team members are notorious for sidestepping or overlooking the problems of group process. Most team members look out for themselves rather than for the team. They are so busy 'doing' that they don't take time to evaluate *how* they're doing it. Sometimes they lack confidence in the team's ability to handle the stress of self-analysis, so they don't force the issue. The result? Nobody calls attention to a dysfunctional process.

Taking the team forward you need to correct this. What's going on inside the team? Analyse its effectiveness. Determine what's missing, what's getting in the way, what needs to happen.

You need a sharp eye plus the nerve to make the team deal with process problems. Regularly stop the team in its tracks. Call a halt long enough to let the team hold a mirror up to itself. Process analysis is as simple as saying, 'Let's look at what's going on now. How do you feel about that? Let's analyse how we're working together as a team.' Make everybody take a hard look at what's happening. Don't let people dodge issues, gloss over sensitive points, or turn the conversation toward mere chit-chat. Make the team face the facts and come up with constructive ideas on how to handle the process problems. Finally, make it clear that each team member is in charge of protecting the team process. Tell everyone to throw the spotlight of attention on behaviour that gets in the way.

Tip

If you put good people in bad systems you get bad results. You have to water the flowers you want to grow.

7. Give people decision-making powers

Enable/empower members of the team. This means sometimes you will simply need to communicate an instruction and they will know the level of authority that they have to act on their own. If they don't know how to do something, they should be coached or trained. Empowerment should enable members of the team to act on local decisions that influence their own work.

Each team member must be given a defined area of functional freedom within which they can exercise their knowledge and skills. Decisions or actions that potentially take an individual or group across their area boundary will of course be subject to your sanction as the team leader and they will be aware of this. But inside the arena the individual must be free, that is enabled/empowered to operate according to their own sanctions.

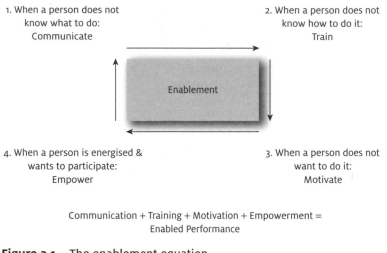

1. When a person does not
know what to do:
Communicate

2. When a person does not
know how to do it:
Train

Enablement

4. When a person is energised &
wants to participate:
Empower

3. When a person does not
want to do it:
Motivate

Communication + Training + Motivation + Empowerment =
Enabled Performance

Figure 3.1   The enablement equation

> **Tip**
>
> It's amazing how much a team can accomplish when it
> does not matter who gets the credit. (Father Stickland,
> 1863)

8. Performance manage with precision

Your role as the leader of the team is to set high standards. Then
defend them. Aim for excellence to build pride, esprit de corps
and cohesiveness. Keep things tightly organised. Don't allow
people to drift back into old routines or habits. Hold team members
accountable for all their assigned tasks. Keep them to their agreed
timetables and deadlines. Don't be vague or fuzzy in laying down
the rules, or in explaining what you want, or inconsistent in
enforcing objectives. If you make as many exceptions as you
do rules, you have no rules.

Always be prepared to back up your words with action. Team members will listen to what you have to say, but their behaviour will be shaped by what you *do*. Keep a high profile. Remember that you have no more powerful way to communicate than by example and you can't lead by example if the team can't see you. This way team members will have confidence in you.

The aim is to ultimately move your team to self-managed status as soon as possible. This means that on a productivity as well as behavioural basis they need to self-regulate. As the team move to this status they should decide what is and isn't acceptable and have this as a formal or informal contract between them. People have to play for the team, not just for themselves. Any half-hearted effort or lack of productivity should be dealt with swiftly by the team itself, and you step in only if you see this process is floundering.

Don't be tempted to micromanage. You have put people together for a specific task or function, so operate on the assumption that they know what they are doing. Check in periodically to make sure they are on track, or ask for updates, but don't hover and intimidate them – it will only make them feel less secure and more apt to make mistakes. Let them know they can come to you for advice or guidance and, if they do, adopt an attitude of benevolence rather than berating them. Get into the habit, though, of encouraging them to come up with their own solutions.

9. Motivate and celebrate

Reward, reward and reward good performance. The intangible rewards you have to offer are limitless:

- **words of encouragement, compliments;**
- **empathy and understanding, a note of appreciation;**
- **stopping to share a cup of coffee, or taking a team member to lunch;**

- giving team members special assignments or more decision-making authority;
- a sincere thank you;
- asking about the family;
- celebrating small victories, soliciting opinions and suggestions;
- listening, really listening;
- a smile, a warm handshake or pat on the back;
- taking someone into your confidence.

Asking for help is gratifying because it validates a person's worth. Caring takes time. It requires that you pay attention to what's happening. Create a supportive team environment – nurture – and watch it bring out the best in people. Show approval and see how it arms the team. When you affirm, you empower. People feel safer, valued and more optimistic. Trust levels increase. Team members are more creative and engage their talents more fully. If you make every member of the team feel special, you'll end up with a very special team.

10. Build communication channels that work

Give the team constant updates. Even no news is news. If you don't regularly update the team, they'll fill in the blanks themselves and you feed the rumour mill by default. Unless you speak for yourself, somebody will speak for you. If you want certain information to stick, keep saying it. If you have to deliver a complex or difficult message, put it in writing.

Since communication travels four times as fast from the top down as from the bottom up, you should put new 'pipelines' in place to carry information to you. If you know what the problems are and hear about them early enough, you can usually fix them. So deputise every team member. Ask them to go looking for problems. Instead of looking for proof that changes are happening or working, search for evidence that they aren't.

Bring your team together often. Talk. Air issues and discuss. Pool everyone's thoughts on how to resolve problems so as to keep everyone 'in the loop'. Invite argument and allow conflict. You'll end up with better solutions. Don't allow differences to be swept under the rug as this will haunt the team later. You won't have a high performance team unless you meet the tough issues head on.

11. Have a plan

Set a clear agenda. Members of the team need a sense of direction *quickly*. Work with them to create specific priorities to help them figure out how to spend their time. The more you include them in the decision-making process the greater their commitment will be.

The action plan sets out the way forward with crystal clear tactical objectives giving the team laser-like focus. Alignment of effort depends on your ability to orient the team and orchestrate a coordinated effort.

Map out new priorities when they are required. Keep them simple and tie them to a specific timetable. Set short-term goals that the team can achieve quickly. Potential resistance can be defused when your instructions are unequivocal and easily understood. Make known your commitment to them and their commitment to achieving the goals. Tell them at the outset that they can expect some mid-course corrections. The agenda will have to be adapted as the situation demands it. But, *always* keep it clear and communicate it constantly.

12. Focus on results

Focus on tangible results. Go for those operational improvements that are most urgently needed. Focus on those things that go straight to the bottom line or that contribute directly to the competitive position. Stake out specific targets. Aim for a few – but ambitious – goals. Go for measurable gains. Make the objectives SMART(ER)

– specific, measurable, achievable, realistic, timed (ethical and rewarded).

Having looked at the key steps for setting up a new team, let's look at other considerations.

How to balance the team

Some interesting research work on teams was carried out by Belbin at the Henley Administration Staff College over a period of several years in the 1970s. He started out with a simple idea that different types of people interact in different ways. The research identified that there are a number of distinctive roles that people play in teams and that the ideal (successful and effective) team is made up of a mix of people who fulfil different roles.

I think it is important to understand different team roles and the contribution they make to the good of the whole in balancing the team. It can help you and those in your team understand both the function of a team and the contribution they individually can make that goes beyond the job description. It also enables everyone to value the differing contributions made by colleagues, and helps you when planning to delegate.

In the matrix in Table 3.1 you will see a brief résumé of the team types that were identified during the research project. (The naming of each role has been changed and amended by Belbin over the years. The roles in the table have been cited in his book, *Team Roles at Work*, 2003.)

Looking at the matrix you can see that Belbin states strengths of contribution in any one of the roles is commonly associated with particular weaknesses. He described these as 'allowable weaknesses'. Let's face it, people are never strong in all nine team roles, however much we like to think of ourselves as 'wonder men or women'!

I think this is a good first-level guide. It is important to recognise that any team is only as good as the sum of its members.

Table 3.1 Team types

Roles	Team Role Contribution	Allowable Weaknesses
Plant	Creative, imaginative, unorthodox, solves difficult problems	Ignores details. Too preoccupied to communicate effectively
Resource investigator	Extrovert, enthusiastic, communicative. Explores opportunities. Develops contacts	Over-optimistic. Loses interest once initial enthusiasm has passed
Coordinator	Mature, confident, a good chairperson. Clarifies goals, promotes decision making, delegates well	Can be seen as manipulative. Delegates personal work
Shaper	Challenging, dynamic, thrives on pressure. Has the drive and courage to overcome obstacles	Can provoke others. Hurts people's feelings
Monitor evaluator	Sober, strategic and discerning. Sees all options. Judges accurately	Lacks drive and ability to inspire others. Overly critical
Teamworker	Cooperative, mild, perceptive and diplomatic. Listens, builds, averts friction, calms the waters	Indecisive in crunch situations. Can be easily influenced
Implementer	Disciplined, reliable, conservative and efficient. Turns ideas into practical actions	Somewhat inflexible. Slow to respond to new possibilities
Completer	Painstaking, conscientious, anxious. Searches out errors and omissions. Delivers on time	Inclined to worry unduly. Reluctant to delegate. Can be a nit-picker

Each member is different but important. Team members don't need to be all the same. In fact, a successful team needs a mix of people, personalities and skills to be successful. An individual may, and often does, exhibit strong tendencies towards multiple roles. Certainly in small teams an individual can play more than one role. In reality, it is not always possible to set up a team with exactly the right mix of individuals. If, however, you think each of the roles represents a team process, then you need to make sure that these processes all occur.

So, for example, taking a few of the characteristics identified above, the term *Plant* was used by Belbin because this type of team member appeared to 'sit in the corner' and not interact a lot, rather like a house plant. Plants are creative, unorthodox and good at generating ideas. For in-depth problem solving, or at the start of a new project, they are an excellent resource to use. They often bear a strong resemblance to the caricature of the 'absent-minded professor', and are not always that good at communicating ideas to others. So you need to tap into their creativity, and draw out information from them by using open questioning techniques – using the words 'who, what, why, where, when and how' to start a sentence.

The *Resource Investigator* will often have a great deal of enthusiasm at the beginning of a project, be a good networker and tap into contacts outside of the team to gather information to bring back for an assignment. When I first moved in to consultancy, there was a researcher in our department who fulfilled this role to a T. She spent a proportion of her time doing classic research at the London Business School, gathering information for consultants. However, a great deal of the information she gathered was through chatting to staff in the coffee room, getting 'grapevine' information to pass around the building about the linkage between the different assignments staff were undertaking, and in turn where there might be cross-selling business opportunities.

Another two roles worth a mention are the *Coordinator* and *Shaper*. Both are leadership roles, and they can be complementary. The Coordinator observes the team and knows the strengths and weaknesses of each person in the team, whereas the Shaper will often be the one who challenges and stimulates discussion – questioning approaches, etc. Too many Shapers in the team, according to Belbin, can lead to conflict, aggravation and in-fighting.

CASE STUDY   Department of Computer Sciences, Virginia Tech

Research has been undertaken by Sallie M Henry and K Todd Stevens, in the Department of Computer Science, Virginia Tech, where they explored the use of Belbin's leadership role to improve team effectiveness (Henry and Stevens, 1999).

They conducted a controlled experiment with senior software engineering students, looking at the use of Belbin's roles from a performance, productivity and team viability point of view. In a laboratory setting, a number of teams were formed that contained a single leader, and others were formed that had no leaders or multiple leaders. The conclusion of the experiment was that a single leader in a team improved team performance over teams having multiple or no leaders. The mean time-to-completion of the leaderless team was significantly greater than the team with leaders.

Finally, the *Completer*. For any major project it is important to have a person who is concerned with accuracy and making sure the layout of documents is perfect. They are happy to check and recheck what is to be delivered, and ensure that the project has achieved its objective.

To summarise, use the 12-step guide for setting up your new team, and remember to get the balance of people right. This can make a world of difference. It can be the difference between failure and success.

Table 3.2

	Rating*
Do members of my team trust me and each other?	
Are my actions consistent with my words?	
Are my team members and I honest with each other?	
Is information readily shared?	
Do my team and I listen effectively to one another?	
Do we address disagreements and other conflicts proactively and responsively?	
Do we value differences? For example, do we value introverted members to the same degree as extroverted members of the team?	
Is the working environment inclusive, engaging and empowering?	
Do I as a manager/team leader foster cooperation and information sharing with other departments or teams?	
Does my team have fun at work? Do we celebrate together as a team?	
Is there anything you would like to add to clarify your response in more detail?	

*Rating: Strongly agree: 5; Agree: 4; Indifferent: 3; Slightly disagree: 2; Strongly disagree: 1

Checklist exercise

A quick monitoring checklist is shown in Table 3.2. Be brave! Pass it to each member of your team and ask them to be honest in their response, rating each item between 1 and 5. Tell them no one will be identified from the responses on the form (you are not planning to analyse each person's writing!) If there is a consistently low score of below 4 in any of the boxes, this is where there is room for improvement.

Checklist for action
- Define a common purpose or team description then set a goal.
- Gain a deeper understanding of what makes your people tick through the use of a behavioural tool or assessment instrument.
- Set up a process that fosters genuine buy-in, commitment and sense of ownership, and encourages responsibility among team members.
- Commit to a 100 per cent open communication environment, where frankness is valued and lack of honesty is not tolerated. Openness must be the norm.

4

Managing the team once formed – motivation and performance management

'They don't seek out the limelight for themselves but challenge, stretch and champion others, giving them the space and support to excel.'
(Tamkin *et al*, 2010)

Introduction

So the members of the team have been selected, and it is your role as the manager/team leader to ensure that outcomes are achieved.

In this chapter we are going to look at performance management, focusing on motivation to begin with. We are then going to explore how you should manage performance on a day-by-day basis, and then in a more formal context through the appraisal process. Important, of course, is how to acknowledge and reward good performance. Poor performance is dealt with in Chapter 7.

Performance management is about doing the right thing and doing things right. It's about achieving stated objectives. This statement just rolls off the tongue and makes it sound so easy. But how often do you go into organisations where you hear people saying 'I've got a lousy manager! He never tells me anything', 'I don't really understand what I am supposed to be doing half the time' or, 'The goalposts keep on changing.' Something is not right somewhere. People are clearly demotivated and poorly managed in each of these situations.

Your job as a manager is to get results through others. A well-motivated team of average players will invariably beat a poorly motivated team of star players. So let's start by looking at motivation.

The art of motivation

You can get a group together and train them in teamwork for weeks but they won't be a team until they have a common understanding of the need to perform. People will only perform to a high standard if they are motivated to do so.

Motivation is the force that makes us do things. This is a result of our individual needs being satisfied (or met) so that we have inspiration to complete the task. These needs vary from person to person: everybody has their individual needs to motivate themselves. How motivated a person is will determine the amount of effort he or she will put into your team or company.

To motivate those in the team, managers need to create a climate of self-motivation that encourages team member development and growth. If you have recruited the right people, they won't be hard to motivate. A team of proactive, motivated self-starters put you right out front, to achieve your goals and financial success.

However, you will still need to invest regular time in motivating and encouraging them.

John Kotter, in *A Force for Change* (1990), writes:

> Motivating people for a short period of time is not that difficult.
> A crisis will often do just that, or a carefully planned celebratory
> event. Keeping people motivated over a long period of time is far
> more difficult. Motivation over time requires that visions and strategies
> be communicated on a continuous basis, not just once or occasionally.
> Communication must go beyond simply informing people, it must
> excite them by connecting to their values.

Why is motivation so important?

For the same reason, that you need a bath or shower every 24 hours! To keep yourself clear from the daily contamination of your environment and to be fresh, clean and feeling great every day! The dictionary defines 'motivation' as:

1. To provide a reason for action.
2. To cause a person to act in a particular way.
3. To stimulate in a way that gets positive results.

The meaning of the word 'energy' in Greek, *energeia*, is 'work activity'. The dictionary definitions are:

1. To have or cause to have energy.
2. To invigorate.
3. To create vital action.
4. To stimulate intense activity.

So what is 'motivational energy'?

It is a creative, positive mindset that results in highly stimulating intense activity. When people are personally motivated, they:

- act with enthusiasm;
- approach life with a positive viewpoint;
- have a strong inner drive to achieve;
- develop powerful inner energy;
- are active;
- get results.

The word 'motivation' is basically made up of two words – *motive* and *action*. For every 'action' we take, there is a 'motive' and a reason for it. The key is to find and develop the right motives (needs, desires, reasons and thoughts) that help a person achieve the right and best actions. But how do we even begin with this?

A fundamental principle of motivation

A US psychologist, A J Maslow, drew a 'pyramid of needs' split into five bands, building up from basic needs for food and shelter to 'personal fulfilment' – the 'icing on the cake'; it is shown in Figure 4.1. This analysis is important for several reasons:

- **It is true of all normal human beings, whatever their personality type or personal situation.**
- **The successive levels are arranged in priority sequence, so if you try to satisfy a high-level need before a lower-level one you are building an unstable situation (all the personal fulfilment in the world will not raise motivation if the individual isn't paid enough to provide adequate food, clothes and housing).**
- **By understanding the needs you can construct reward packages, including non-salary benefits and intangible benefits, tailored to the individual whose motivation you wish to raise.**
- **It provides a quick checklist you can use to screen out potentially counterproductive initiatives (those that cause deprivation at lower levels).**

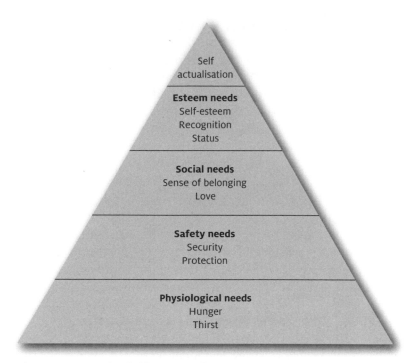

Figure 4.1   Maslow's hierarchy of needs

The five levels are:

1. *Physiological needs:* basic food, clothing, shelter, etc for the individual and his or her dependants, normally catered for through the basic salary.
2. *Safety needs:* ranging from physical security to long-term financial security. No one can be highly motivated if their concentration and commitment are distracted by chronic fear. In today's world many aspects of this level of security are provided by insurance, pension schemes and the like.
3. *Social needs or belonging:* most of us need to feel accepted as full and equal members of the human race. We satisfy much of this need through our families and networks of relationships, reflecting our particular interests, religion,

politics and culture but, given that we spend around a
third of our adult lives at work, a sense of 'belonging' to
work-related groups has an important bearing on our
attitude to our colleagues and employers.

4. *Esteem:* by and large we try reasonably hard to do a good
job, and take pride in the fruits of our labour; we take even
more pride and pleasure in seeing these appreciated by
others, particularly our superiors. The esteem of others
raises our image amongst our peers and differentiates us
within the group while reinforcing our sense of belonging
and value to the group. It also acts as a spur to greater efforts
in future.

5. *Self-actualisation or self-fulfilment:* that feeling of pleasure
from 'a job well done', whether it is a neatly mown lawn, a
beautifully designed power station or an ordinary repetitive
task performed efficiently and effectively.

As already discussed, the needs at the top of this list take
priority. These must be satisfied before you can take more
than a fleeting pleasure from having lower priority, higher
'quality' needs satisfied. However, once they are satisfied they
are virtually ignored. A salary adequate to keep ourselves and our
dependants in an acceptable lifestyle allows us to start worrying
about maintaining that lifestyle, and security takes a higher
profile. Once these two 'inwards-looking' needs are satisfied
we begin to look around ourselves, and our place in the group
starts to become important, and so on. In principle, a regular
salary plus benefits can take care of the physiological and safety
needs.

Meanwhile the satisfaction of needs, particularly at the
higher levels, has an iterative element. When we are toddlers,
the ability to read 'the cat sat on the mat' brings great
satisfaction; a year or two later we need to read a complete
book to get the same thrill. To borrow a phrase from the field
of athletics, we gain self-fulfilment by constantly achieving
new 'personal bests', stretching our talents to meet ever more
ambitious goals.

How does this apply in the workplace?

It is nowadays widely held that the need for self-fulfilment and the need for esteem or recognition are amongst the most important motivating factors in the workplace. However, there is less agreement as to whether the sources of the satisfaction are intrinsic, in other words within the actual work itself, or whether they lie in the environment, the quality of relationships between managers and employees, and the atmosphere within the organisation.

If you think about this for a moment, it soon becomes clear that these are two sides of a single coin. No matter how satisfying our work, if it is conducted in a sour atmosphere we will soon lose our will to excel. Similarly, if we are set to work on uncongenial tasks, poorly suited to our personal skill set and personality, then no matter how positive the surroundings, we will soon begin to fret and stop giving of our best. As a rule of thumb it is important that people are set tasks at which they believe they can excel, and the work should be located in a positively charged atmosphere that helps people to succeed. Success has a knock-on effect. Those that are motivated will help motivate others and generally reinforce a positive feedback loop for the benefit of the team and of course, ultimately, the organisation.

The essential point is that we are all individuals, with different personalities and personal needs that overlay Maslow's pyramid. You can see this even at the basic needs level. Imagine two very similar people with similar skills doing similar work. One might have a non-working partner and three or four school-age children; the other might be a bachelor with a penchant for mountaineering. The father will need a family home, the other a small apartment; the father will need a high income to pay the myriad of bills, the other might be happier with a smaller salary but more time in the mountains. It follows that, as a team leader, you can make use of even the most basic needs to increase your team members' motivation, in this case by devising creative 'cafeteria' rewards schemes, which allow individuals to make up a total package that most closely satisfies their personal needs and aspirations.

More generally, our personalities differ. At one extreme we find hermits, who are perfectly happy gaining satisfaction from their work with minimal human intervention; at the other we find people who are happy only when interacting with other people. Most of us are somewhere in between, able to spend periods concentrating on work but needing social interaction.

It is part of the team leader's job to analyse the job/people make-up of tasks and then to assign them to individuals whose personalities most closely approach the required mixture. Much unhappiness is caused by failure to observe this simple rule, usually because we are so concerned with matching the technical knowledge or practical skill requirements that we forget that we are, for example, asking a 'hermit' to front customer services, a job for which, no matter how excellent his or her product knowledge, he or she is temperamentally quite unsuitable. The impact on the individual is to provoke fear and hence undermine his or her need for security, thereby breaking the 'Maslow rule' that high-priority needs must be satisfied first.

Another important aspect of this theme of personal needs as satisfied through the workplace is that people grow up and, as they mature, their interests evolve. This is part of the iterative process of seeking new challenges when old challenges have been exhausted. As a team leader you must recognise when people are ready to move on, and help them prepare for the migration by introducing them to appropriate training and opportunities in areas for which they are now temperamentally and intellectually ready.

For example, many young people find computers fascinating in themselves, and gain rich fulfilment from programming. For some, programming seems never to grow dull, since there is always a new problem to solve or better techniques to be designed; but many people 'grow out of' programming. Where do they go? There is no one simple solution, again since we are all different individuals. Options (the directions do not imply value judgements) include:

- **forwards towards systems and applications design;**
- **back towards manufacture, engineering and design of the hardware;**

- directly towards sales or marketing of the machines or the software;
- sideways towards training and customer support;
- upwards towards management of programmers.

In the course of a career, either as a result of natural development or of an inspired manager asking you to use existing skills to tackle a 'new' problem or aspect of the business, you can pass through many different phases, adding new skills and developing a higher-level understanding of the products and their capabilities. This also adds more value to the employer's business.

Another important personal need is increased responsibility, since the granting of responsibility is evidence of esteem. We know this from personal experience: when we begin to work at a new type of task our teacher or manager hangs over our shoulders to correct our errors and guide us round pitfalls. Soon we feel confident enough to work without such close supervision, and begin to resent it, feeling that 'They don't trust me' and that we are held in low esteem. If, on the other hand, supervision is tapered off or withdrawn just before the manager is fully confident that the new lessons have been fully assimilated, then the message is 'Wow! They trust me, even though I am not really quite ready' – a powerful stimulant to motivation.

Traditionally, in highly stratified organisations with many management layers, adding responsibility was easily done by an annual or biennial promotion. Nowadays more subtle approaches are needed, such as:

- withdrawal of supervision;
- 'bigger' jobs of the same type;
- wider responsibility within the same job (eg adding stock ordering to an assembly team or making a customer service team partly responsible for defining product enhancements);
- adding training and supervision of new recruits to the 'doing' part of the job.

These methods of injecting additional responsibility into teams doing basically repetitive work will be familiar to students of Japanese management techniques. There are many motives for following this path, but demonstrating trust in and raising the self-esteem and self-fulfilment (and hence the motivation) of the work group is an essential element.

Managing performance

When looking at how you should manage the performance of team members it is important to consider the bigger picture. You need to understand how performance standards should bear a straight-line relationship to what your organisation has set out to achieve. Figure 4.2 clarifies this.

As can be seen, your team's 'key performance indicators' must be related directly to your organisation's aims, above your team in the hierarchy, and the team members responsible for them, below. They are therefore firmly *in context* and can correctly determine what training, resources, leadership and processes are required – even what recruitment policy should be pursued.

Making obvious the connection between organisation and individuals is crucial. Too many team members are 'lost' in the sense that they are not aligned with the organisation's vision and mission. This is a mistake. Today's paradox is that just as employees can expect less loyalty from organisations, these organisations are more than ever dependent on high level performance from employees. One way to generate loyalty is to give your team members clear sight lines to the organisation's vision and keep them informed of the personal and team contribution they are making to deliver this.

What's the purpose of my job?

Every team member must be clear about how they contribute towards the overall team effort, and how the team's results turn the organisation's vision and mission into reality.

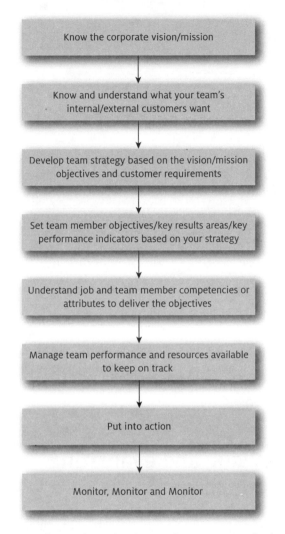

Know the corporate vision/mission

Know and understand what your team's internal/external customers want

Develop team strategy based on the vision/mission objectives and customer requirements

Set team member objectives/key results areas/key performance indicators based on your strategy

Understand job and team member competencies or attributes to deliver the objectives

Manage team performance and resources available to keep on track

Put into action

Monitor, Monitor and Monitor

Figure 4.2   Setting and monitoring performance standards

We often advise team leaders to create a team job description. Most job descriptions, if we are honest, focus on activities and behaviours. The team job description must focus on activities, behaviours *and results*. For example, if a responsibility in a job description is to 'produce monthly reports' the question to ask is 'In order to do what?' The point is to keep asking the question,

'In order to do what' until you finally reach a concrete result, which contributes towards overall organisation success. (Remember the use of 'concrete' in the last chapter? It means what exactly, and by when and contains a figure.)

Key Results Areas (KRAs)

Key results areas flow from individual or team job descriptions. KRAs contribute towards clarifying *how we should (as a team) be spending our time.* For the team's strategy to succeed, all team members must achieve specific results which, when accumulated, ensure that all strategy elements are delivered. KRAs are a summary of those key factors of individual or the team's job that are vital for the team's success. KRAs must be monitored, at a minimum, each month. Otherwise, divergences from your strategy may occur.

If you have difficulty identifying your KRAs, ask yourself the following question: what are the major aspects of the team's work that could go wrong? You might answer, 'We don't realise our sales target'; 'We use up our resources'; 'Too many customers complain' or, 'We don't complete our reports on time.' These can be translated into the following KRAs: sales, finance, customer service, and monthly reports.

Reviewing and evaluating performance

Your role as a manager is to communicate your organisation's goals in terms that members of the team can understand and will support on a personal level. Effective team leadership promotes the concept of teamwork by showing them 'What's in it for you'.

In your management role you need to be able to not only communicate effectively, but also to boost morale, motivate and develop others. Performance reviews will be on a day-to-day basis and more formally during a performance review – an appraisal.

This is usually undertaken on an annual basis, first to review a team member's previous performance, and then to establish specific goals and objectives for the following year, as well as to discuss career interests and development needs and requirements.

Methods for giving and receiving feedback

The idea behind any form of evaluation is to show the person concerned the value he or she brings to the team and the organisation – what his or her strengths are. On the flip side, evaluation also can highlight areas of concern and where there is room for improvement.

The purpose of feedback is to either maintain or to change performance in order to keep individuals on track to achieve their objectives/work goals. Of course it is much easier to give negative feedback if you are a team leader/manager and giving the information to someone that reports in to you. If you feel it is important to give feedback to your own manager, choose your time and place carefully! A neutral venue, not his or her office, or during an annual review is best.

Using a formalised methodology you could use 360-degree feedback. As the name implies it is getting feedback from all those around you that you link with on a regular basis. The process involves those who are to be evaluated selecting a group of colleagues and stakeholders who they work with, and giving them documentation to complete. The type of information that will be collected will indicate the perception those completing the questionnaires have about their colleague and how he or she acts in certain situations, style of communication, creative and strategic approach. The candidate being evaluated can also within the 360-degree feedback have the opportunity to name his or her replacement for succession planning purposes.

But much of our working life is not based on written documentation being given to us. Feedback, nine times out of 10, is a verbal review or exchange of information. For the person giving the feedback on performance, what is important? Let's take the example of you giving a person a task to do – say writing a report, or assessing the viability of going to market with a new product or service. In this situation you will either give:

Motivational feedback – telling the person his or her performance has been noted and giving him or her the impetus to repeat this type of performance again. Give it as soon after the event as possible.

Or:

Development feedback – indicating to the person that you are looking for improvements. Get him or her to make suggestions as to how he or she might tackle the task/situation in a different way. Get him or her to think through options; don't just come up with the solution yourself.

If you have to correct behaviour this is a totally different kettle of fish. What are the key factors to bear in mind?

Tips: Feedback on behaviour

Feedback equals information. Feedback is a critical piece of communication in any successful organisation. There is no 'right' way to give feedback, but here are some tips and techniques to help you make informed decisions about the best time, place and intent with which to give constructive feedback:

- **Feedback should be given any time an individual thinks a behaviour should be reinforced or needs to be corrected.**
- **Providing feedback should freely and openly flow between all team members.**
- **Give feedback to ensure it is received in a constructive way.**
- **Give constructive feedback to enable improvement and growth.**

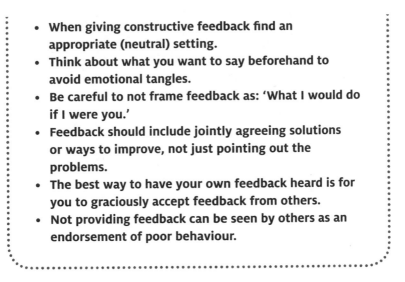

- When giving constructive feedback find an appropriate (neutral) setting.
- Think about what you want to say beforehand to avoid emotional tangles.
- Be careful to not frame feedback as: 'What I would do if I were you.'
- Feedback should include jointly agreeing solutions or ways to improve, not just pointing out the problems.
- The best way to have your own feedback heard is for you to graciously accept feedback from others.
- Not providing feedback can be seen by others as an endorsement of poor behaviour.

Now let's move on to formally reviewing the performance of a member of the team.

The annual performance review or appraisal process

Appraisal is important for both the team leader and the person in the team being reviewed. It measures how a number of factors have changed since a previous appraisal:

- how well the appraisee has performed against previously agreed objectives;
- what planned or unplanned developments have occurred in the appraisee's skill set;
- how the appraisee's ambitions and expectations have changed.

An appraisal session is usually an interview with a colleague you already know. Begin the meeting with a positive attitude. This means that the appraisee details his or her perception of their performance first. You must learn to control any eagerness to judge others and let them evaluate themselves first. After all, whose opinions do we all prefer most?

The mistakes managers can make during the appraisal process

1. Not addressing in a timely manner the problem areas that were identified in the previous appraisal session

As the person reviewing performance you should have been monitoring the problem(s) that had been identified, what actions were agreed, and what results were achieved at the time that they occurred, not just at the annual formal appraisal meeting. During this meeting you can acknowledge the status and outcomes in a sign-off capacity, but not take valuable time out of the meeting to review the historic resolution of a problem area that occurred several months ago. This means that during the appraisal process SMART objectives are agreed to assist the appraisee in improving his or her performance at the pace that the role demands.

2. Feedback being too general, with no concrete facts

You need to give specific examples of where you considered performance was good as well as where it was poor. It is a good idea to document this as you progress through the year, not just recall facts during the meeting.

3. Not getting the balance right

Only focusing on underperformance, not giving positive strokes as well. How often people wish they could avoid the 'dreaded annual appraisal', because their manager only tells them what they have done wrong, not what they have done right!

4. The action improvement plan not being implemented

If underperformance has been identified, this can mean there has been no planning of resources to support the person who needs to correct his or her behaviour so they don't do the same things again. This can also apply to people who have performed well: they need to have the bar raised, and an improvement plan put in place to monitor their progress.

5. Rewarding misaligned achievements

People can be very enthusiastic about a particular part of their workload and outperform in this area. However, rewards and grading of performance are not just about effort and input during the year. Not all good work can be rewarded. You need to be able to articulate that what the person is doing needs to be aligned to the company's goals. They need to be focused on top line key performance indicators.

6. Lack of feedback with regard to your performance as a manager

Performance reviews should not just be a one-way passage. There needs to be time during the meeting to get feedback from them as to how they see your performance as a manager, and what help and support they might need from you.

7. Interruptions and lack of privacy

When you are undertaking a performance review you need to turn off mobiles, and make sure you are not sitting next to or facing your PC when e-mails might be arriving thick and fast. An uninterrupted space is critical, particularly if you have to give corrective feedback.

Rewards

Rewards are typically based on the carrot and stick principle. If you perform well you get a reward, but if you underperform you are punished – there's no reward. Rewards can certainly concentrate the mind when there are a simple set of rules and a clear destination – a goal.

As long as the task involved is purely a mechanical skill, bonuses work. The issue, however, is that in Western Europe, Asia, the United States/Canada and Australia, white-collar workers in all sorts or roles and sectors are doing less of the routine work. Many of their tasks have been automated or outsourced. Their work responsibilities have expanded to thinking through challenges, opportunities and problem solving, and this involves working far more with the right side of their brain. The challenges and problems that have to be resolved are complex, mystifying, surprising and not obvious. Think of your own job: this is probably the case.

The author, Daniel Pink of TEDtalks Director, gave a presentation on 'The surprising science of motivation' in 2011. He believes that rewards don't work in this context. He quotes research undertaken by the London School of Economics which found that once a task called for even rudimentary cognitive skills, a larger reward led to poorer performance. The findings from this research showed that intrinsic motivation was considered more of a reward; in other words, doing things because they mattered, or people liked them, or felt they were part of something important.

Of course a fair pay structure is of fundamental importance, but Pink quotes three factors to be of importance:

1. autonomy – people directing their own lives and workload;
2. mastery – the desire to be better and better;
3. purpose – doing something that matters: the yearning to do what we do in the service of something larger than ourselves.

Organisational award schemes

In my years as a consultant I have noticed the following issues regarding reward schemes:

- **Recognition should be about receiving thanks/praise for a job well done.**
- **Recognition does not happen enough and does not generally extend beyond the immediate team/line manager.**
- **Existing organisation communication methods – internal newspaper, intranet, team meetings, etc – should support personal recognition.**
- **Reward is a personal issue – a 'one prize fits all' approach would not be satisfactory.**
- **Team members should be rewarded for good behaviours associated with positive teamworking, sharing of best practice, etc as well as results.**
- **Reward and recognition must be timely and related to specific incidents.**

CASE STUDY   Google and autonomy

At Google the engineers can spend 20 per cent of their time doing whatever they want, experimenting. They have autonomy over the task, the time factor, the techniques they use, and the team they select to help them. This radical approach has led to the development of half their new products, such as Gmail and Google News, being developed in this 20 per cent of their time.

CASE STUDY John Lewis

John Lewis employees received a whopping 18 per cent of their salary as a bonus in 2007 – equivalent to nine weeks' pay. The company, with its unusual business structure, had enjoyed such a good year that it could afford to pay out £155 million in bonuses alone.

Media coverage at the time asked how much of the John Lewis Partnership's success was down to the buy-in of the workforce, who have an even stronger vested interest in going the extra mile than staff in more conventional relationships with their employers. Could it be that, contrary to the popular perception that an employee-owned organisation is slow and cumbersome, sharing ownership is the best way to motivate a workforce?

Employee-owned businesses deliver long term. In the mid 1990s, the firm's performance was less startling, partly because of significant restructuring and investment. This included the purchase of buy.com, an internet retail platform, which took time to bed down. Eventually, John Lewis developed this into johnlewis.com, a significant driver of John Lewis's success today.

Putting even more weight behind the idea that engaged staff are harder workers, the company has now launched a new scheme, BonusSave, which allows staff to invest all or part of their bonuses, and save Income Tax and National Insurance on this investment, provided that it is left in the plan for five years.

In an environment where talented staff are difficult to find and even harder to hang on to, innovative staff loyalty programmes like these are on the increase.

(Norris, 2007)

Checklist for action

- Review your rewards scheme to ensure it increases your staff motivation by devising a 'cafeteria' type rewards scheme, which allows individuals to make up a total package that most closely satisfies their personal needs and aspirations.
- Make sure team member Key Results Areas are monitored, at a minimum, monthly. Otherwise, divergences from your strategy may occur.
- Every meeting with team members should be an opportunity for improvement and motivation. This means meetings should be a mini-appraisal, encouraging actions where appropriate and agreeing a plan.
- Check to see if your reward schemes align with staff member needs.

5

Managing the team once formed – communication, meetings, influencing and projects

Introduction

Let's look at four other activities that you will inevitably have to undertake if you lead a team. You are the communication messenger, you run and will attend meetings, you will need to influence others and manage projects. Now all four of these activities are of importance, but what needs to be considered to ensure that they don't take a disproportionate amount of your time, and you can't get on with 'your day job' – in other words your own personal activities and projects?

First, in your role as a communication messenger you need to be very clear about the nature of information that you have to pass on, and assess on a regular basis if you are using the most effective forms of communication. A hidden part of your communication role is to network and find out off-the-record information from colleagues that might have a direct impact on the work of your team. For example, when is new funding from a government body going to be in place, how reliable is a particular client who might be using another service in your organisation at coming up with funds for research or development? Have they found this client is good at 'talking the talk' – saying that funding will be available and then not coming through with it in the time frame they have indicated it? So, in your role as a communication messenger you not only need to be able to gain, for want of a better word, unpublished information, but also influence others to come around to your point of view. You can't build this activity into a time slot each day; this form of activity is not robotic! It is part of the hidden agenda of your role. Tom Peters reckons that 75 per cent of a middle manager's job should be spent on horizontal relationships to speed up relationships in the middle of the organisation.

Your role as a communication messenger

Your role as a team leader is to act as a communicator between senior management and members of your team. It's interesting that you can sometimes find that people with a specialist skill, for example someone in technology, is not that interested in progressing into a team leader or management role. They wish to stay focused in their primary area of expertise and not have to deal with disseminating information, or needing to be a 'political' operator within the organisation in order to get cooperation from others that they have to link with on a regular basis.

Working on the assumption that you are happy to be the leader of a team, what do you need to assess with regard to your role as a communication messenger?

Exercise: Assessing your role as a communication messenger

Go through each of the bullet points below to assess your strengths and weaknesses:

- **What is the nature of information that I have to pass on to those in my team?**
- **What communication methodology do I usually use, and is this the most effective way?**
- **Do I balance collecting information with taking action? Have I got the balance right? Am I prone to waiting for all the information to be at my fingertips and then become a bottleneck in my organisation? Or do I tend to act prematurely before enough information is in place?**
- **Am I inclined to keep information to myself because disseminating it is time-consuming or inconvenient?**
- **In what areas is my knowledge weakest and how can I get others to provide me with the information I require?**
- **How can I use my network of contacts effectively to get information when I need it?**
- **Do I spend enough time building network contacts so that I can get 'off the record' information in a timely manner?**
- **Are the meetings that I set up being as effective as I would like them to be?**

This last bullet point needs to be explored in more detail.

Running meetings

Meetings not only take time; they also have an underlying cost. There is the direct cost of bringing people together and holding the meeting itself, plus the lost time for those involved not doing their normal work. It follows that meetings should be carefully planned and executed efficiently.

There are going to be some meetings where, for example, information is simply being passed on about a new product or service, or new working practices. There will be a degree of inter- action – questions and answers between the deliverer and audience. Likewise you will probably have in place a weekly (or even daily) operational team meeting with a similar format. Where there needs to be more thought and preparation is when you are involved with setting up and chairing a more formal meeting, so let's look at this in more detail.

Checklist for making more formal meetings work

1. Invitations should contain the names of all those invited, the venue (with a map and details of parking facilities and public transport, if necessary), the date, start and end times and the agenda with overall objectives and item-specific objectives. Anyone making a presentation should be identified and all participants should be asked to make relevant preparations.

2. Most people find that it is easier to digest information from the written word rather than just listening to a person speak, so all formal presentations should be circulated to participants long enough beforehand for them to read and digest the information. This is

obviously based on a presentation that is more than just a few key words!

3. Agenda items should be listed in order of priority. Put the urgent and important matters at the top of the agenda, as this should give those attending the impetus to be punctual at the start of the meeting, plus people will also be fresh and alert.

4. If individuals are not needed for all items, juggle the list so they can arrive late or leave early.

5. Don't have an 'Any other business' (AOB) item. If someone has something to contribute that is relevant to an agenda item, that is the time when they should speak. AOB is an opportunity for waffle, for time wasting and for riding of irrelevant personal hobby horses.

6. Meetings must have concrete/SMART objectives – usually agreeing actions or changes – and these should either be achieved, or conclusions drawn as to why not and what should be done next.

7. Mobiles should be turned off during the meeting, and clarification of break times highlighted for people to pick up and respond to messages.

How to chair a meeting

If you are chairing the meeting it is essential to set the correct 'tone' right from the start. This means starting at the pre-advised time of commencement, not 10 or 15 minutes later because a couple of people are late. Bang on time: 'Good day, ladies and gentlemen. Thank you for coming in today to discuss the main subject matter. Our first item is x. You have all seen the papers'. Summarise the objectives and answer any questions raised by the papers – and off you go.

Keep the objectives in mind and 'Go for the close' on each topic as quickly as possible. Some people make little prompt cards for each item with two or three phrases to represent the main decisions to be taken or questions answered, and use them to keep discussions on track. Make sure everyone understands and agrees with (or has been overruled but accepts) the conclusions and that they are recorded accurately on a 'Protocol' sheet before moving to the next topic. This sheet should include what actions are to be taken, by whom and by when. Get the collected Protocols photocopied and distributed before the meeting breaks up.

The agenda should ideally have a time limit for each subject. If you make up time this will allow a little latitude for particularly contentious items or, better still, you can all go back to work (or home) a few minutes earlier. Finish by the appointed time, even if this means dropping the lowest priority agenda items. People often have other appointments/meetings which cannot easily (or politely) be delayed, or trains/planes to catch, and an overrun early in the morning can cause chaos for the rest of the day.

Sometimes there is a threat of overrun because it became evident during the meeting that an additional topic really needs to be considered. Ideally, put it on the agenda for the next meeting or convene a special meeting restricted to just the relevant people. At worst adjourn the present meeting for 20 minutes to allow some preparation time and then restart. However, the primary purpose of distributing working papers ahead of the meeting is to ensure that this sort of problem doesn't arise, since the need for extra discussion should be foreseen.

After the meeting

Get the minutes typed up and ideally circulated within 24 hours. This sends a positive message and reinforces the need for action. The Protocol recording specific actions should be appended to the minutes. These documents should be distributed to all attendees plus those who were invited but could not attend. Specific sections could also be distributed to interested parties.

If you called the meeting then the work described in the Protocol sheets is presumably necessary to enable you to meet your own objectives. So follow up. Diarise the deadline dates, and remind yourself to check progress a few days before the deadlines (or earlier/more often as the case dictates).

Write a special note to anyone who had to do more onerous work or travel a distance, thanking them for their input. It boosts morale and does your personal 'image' no harm.

Getting what you need and want from others – being an influencer

There are so many ways that you need to influence others in your working environment. It could be your boss (during training programmes I usually find this is where most people want to focus!), your peers, people in other teams, or those who report to you.

What do I mean by influence? One definition says it is the process by which you persuade others to follow your advice or suggestion. I like to define it as *the act or power of producing an effect without any apparent exertion of force or direct exercise of command.* It is getting what you need and/or want, and sustaining and/or enhancing the relationship. It is not manipulation, coercion, or command and control.

There are formal ways that you can have an impact on others. One way could be through the creation of a cross-functional team. This might be for developing a new product or the introduction of a new service you are offering to a client. It could be for ongoing problem-solving processes, or quality improvement activities. Equally well, you might need to influence a person on a one-to-one basis using a communication methodology that is effective, or build a 'web of influence' for mustering help from colleagues. So let's look at each of these approaches:

The formal approach

If we look at a typical situation, many technical people have to face: sales staff in the organisation selling a new product or service to clients without bearing in mind the consequence that this will have on the technical personnel and their workload. These staff will not only have to maintain and support the current range of products/services but also be able to incorporate the additional work created by the new business.

How have 'best practice' organisations gone about getting over this problem?

CASE STUDY   Research by the Design Council in the UK

In the Spring of 2008, the Design Council in the UK undertook extensive research of 11 of the world's leading companies – including BT, Yahoo!, Starbucks, Lego, Sony, Virgin Airlines and Microsoft. The aim of this project was to offer information and ideas for other companies to help them strengthen their brands and gain competitive advantage in their own fields of business.

This research focused specifically on the design element, and innovation was one of the core brand values in all of the companies that made them 'stand out from the crowd'. Interesting though, and relevant to the problem situation indicated above, the other factor that the research highlighted was the level of cooperation and interaction between designers and people working in other parts of the business, including engineering and manufacturing. At Lego (the world's sixth largest toymaker) for example, the designers have to be able to speak fluently about the commercial implications of their design decisions. At Xerox, designers are well versed in the analysis methods and processes used by their engineering colleagues, and at Microsoft, at the development stage of new products or services, they put together a cross-functional team of user researchers, engineers, product managers, as well as designers at the initial design stage.

It was not just the fact that cross-functional teams were set up at an early stage that came through in the findings of the report: it was the fact that designers had shown a 'get up and go' attitude in seeking out ways of being involved in the wider business.

(Clark, 2008)

For those of you from a technical background: are you being proactive enough in seeking out ways to be more involved at an early stage in the cycle, when sales staff are in initial discussions with the client about a new product or service? Do cross-functional teams get created at an early enough stage for you to have an impact? Are you asking the right questions, flagging up your concerns about service levels?

I'm not suggesting that you be a 'killjoy' for sales staff, but make them aware of what is required once a new business comes on line. Sales staff are very conscious that if the after-sales service is not up to scratch the client will bear this in mind during their next buying cycle. This could result in the client not even considering your organisation to pitch for new business.

CASE STUDY   Novellus, San Jose California

Semiconductor equipment maker Novellus, based in San Jose in California, has a history of not only getting internal groups together at the design stage to form cross-functional teams, but also includes its suppliers. It has been able to implement 'Lean' production processes for new product releases, instead of just existing ones, thanks to this involvement. This has led to sustainable competitive advantages, including improved credibility with customers due to shorter time-to-market, predictable completion dates, and successful launches.

(Atkinson, 2008)

Communication methodology

You are the vehicle for ideas from your team to reach senior management and in turn for strategic information to be passed on to your team. The effectiveness of your team is heavily dependent on your ability to influence your manager or superiors.

When you need to put a proposition together for approval, for example the development of a new range of services, you must be rational in your explanation of ideas and present *benefits* to senior management. Your proposals or plans should be complete, not piecemeal and, if appropriate, use comparative or quantitative analysis to win their support. You might also use surveys, actual incidents or interviews with stakeholders.

If at first you don't succeed, don't give up! You need to be persistent. Ask for the support of other internal and external people who senior management will listen to. If you can get your hands on the information, show where the same idea has worked elsewhere, and with what results. If you are successful in pushing through an idea or a particularly challenging project you will gain respect from others. Success breeds success – and you and your team should get given the better assignments in the future.

Building a 'web of influence'

'To effectively communicate we must realise that we are all different in the way we perceive the world and use this understanding as a guide to our communication with others.' (Anthony Robbins, US adviser to leaders)

As a team leader, your role is no longer based on knowledge, skill sets and your technical abilities alone. You need to be able to influence others by building a 'web of influence' around you in order, for example, to be able to gain funds for projects/resources, or ensure the right people join your team.

So what do I mean by a 'web of influence'? People throughout your organisation, and also colleagues in other companies, can all make a contribution to working activities – sharing knowledge, informal advice, 'political' information about who are the real power brokers to get action.... You need to invest time and effort in developing these networks. Obviously a mentor can help you in certain situations, but there are a whole range of areas when you might need to call on others for help. This can be as simple as calling in a favour (can a colleague from another team help you put together the information packs for a conference?), through to chatting about a situation that has occurred where you believe undue duress has been put on you, which in your eyes has moved into bullying or harassment. What should you do? How should you go about handling this?

If you are asking favours from people there needs to be a degree of exchange – give and take in the situation. You support them in informal ways as well; it can't be a one-way street.

Ways to build a network of contacts include:

- **volunteer to be part of a committee;**
- **secondment;**
- **ask to visit another department or team for the day to see how they operate;**
- **go out with a member of the sales team for a client visit, and gain a better understanding of what they have to face;**
- **invite people from other teams to come into your team for the day to see the issues your team have to face;**
- **develop relationships with decision makers in other industry sectors, either in a comparable role to yours or at a more senior level.**

It's important to keep the communication flow open with those in your network. Drop them an informal line periodically, or send them an article you see that may be pertinent to their area of activity. Be seen to be giving, not just taking.

The concept of networking in the internet age has now been enhanced by people using social networking sites such as Facebook or LinkedIn. I find this methodology has its benefits – you can get to know what your business colleagues are doing at the click of a mouse at any time of day or night. On the minus side though, I have found that people can be very good at wanting to take – in other words they use your business contacts for their own advantage, and are not necessarily that forthcoming in giving.

Managing a project

The fourth part of your job will be to manage projects. So many projects can flounder – go over budget or not achieve their objectives. I am going to suggest a good robust method of running your projects, almost as a tick box exercise to help you keep on track.

So what is a project? As Bonnie Biafore says in her book, *On Time! On Track! On Target!* a project is a one-time job with specific goals, a clear-cut starting and ending date, and in most cases a budget.

Projects can be various shapes and sizes, from the small and straightforward to extremely large and highly complex. A 'task' does not necessarily have to be called a 'project' for project management methods to be very useful in its planning and implementation. Even the smallest task can benefit from the use of a well-chosen project management technique or tool, especially in the planning stage. Any task that requires some preparation to achieve a successful outcome will probably be done better by using the methodology described below.

Before moving on, let's bear in mind that a methodology is not enough for a project to be successful. There are important personal interactions that need to be borne in mind.

Tips: People considerations during a project

- Great projects are about understanding the end users' needs and motivations. Usually you will have been given a term of reference, which gives you an overview of the project and clarifies the issues to be addressed. Once you have this you will need to ask questions to understand who will benefit, how they will benefit, and also how this project will interface with other projects. Ask open-ended questions – in other words ones that can't be answered by 'yes/no', to encourage the person you are speaking to to open up.

- To really understand the scope of the project you need to listen and read the hidden message that might not overtly be voiced. I repeat *listen* – remember you have two ears and one mouth and use them in that proportion.

- Be a skilful questioner. Start sentences with 'who, what, where, when or how' to get a person talking. As you draw out everything you need to know, recap your interpretation of the information until both parties are in mutual agreement.

- With major projects the terms of reference are often distributed to quite a large audience. If at all possible, check with someone beforehand to ensure that the document contains the right 'tone' to appeal to the final audience, and to pick up on any omissions or unclear points. A mainly technical audience would obviously expect quite a lot of technical in-depth information, whereas a non-technical audience wants an overview of the technical aspects and are more interested (and persuaded) by a business-oriented presentation that concentrates on showing them how the project will help them overcome their business problems and become more effective in meeting their objectives.

- It is important to plan the project with the team so that their contribution and commitment are included and developed. Each task should be reviewed by one member of the team who should report on the feasibility, risks, resources and time frame under their control. For a large project the review might take all day (or several days), with each team member making a presentation to the project manager in turn. The project manager must draw all the information together and present the plan to the project team for review. Only when the team has signed up for the plan should it be presented to the project sponsor for authorisation. Bringing your people with you through involvement is critical during a project. If people in the project team have not bought into the first phase, your project is doomed from the start.

Using a 'belt and braces' methodology for managing projects

Now let's move on to the methodology itself. This might look at first glance like quite a lengthy and comprehensive scenario, but unless you have a good road map to take you forward it is very easy to lose your way during a project, and come in late or way over budget. So here we go.

Initiate or get started

You have to bear in mind the need to develop a solid business case for any project you undertake. Ensure you obtain senior management's agreement before you even start. This might seem glaringly obvious, but I have heard only too often that many projects

Figure 5.1   Managing projects

are started without a firm reason or rationale. By working on and developing a business case you will identify whether it is worth taking forward. Ensure your project fits with the key organisational or departmental agenda. If not, why do it? Make sure you stick to priority projects. Then:

1. Carry out a risk analysis at a high level at the initiation stage. Avoid going into great detail here – aim for an overview focusing on the key risks.
2. Identify at this early stage the key stakeholders. Consider how much you need to consult or involve them at the business case stage. Seek advice if necessary from senior managers.
3. Involve finance people in putting the business case together. They can be great allies in helping crunch the numbers, which should give credibility to your business case.

Hint

Ensure you have the buy-in of senior managers for your project. You will need to work hard to influence upwards and get their support.

Defining your project

Produce a written project definition statement (sometimes called a PID). This document is 'your contract' to carry out the project and should be circulated to key stakeholders. Use the project definition statement to prevent creep, where people come along to ask you to do more and more, and the project gets bigger by the day. Also use it to prevent your going beyond the scope of the project through its use in the review process. Recognise early in the life of the project what is driving the initiative. Is it a drive to improve quality, reduce costs or hit a particular deadline? You can only have one of these. Discuss with the project sponsor what is driving the project and ensure you stick to this throughout. Keep 'the driver' in mind, especially when you monitor and review. Then:

1. Identify in detail what will and will not be included in the project scope. Avoid wasting time by working on those areas that should not be included – this should have been identified in the PID.
2. Get the team involved with identifying the tasks and work breakdown. Identify who fulfils which roles in your project. Document them on the PID. Include a paragraph to show what each person does.
3. Identify who has responsibility for what in the project, for example, project communication is the responsibility of 'AD' or whoever. This helps reduce doubt early in the life of the project.
4. If you have the opportunity to create a project team from scratch, think 'team selection' – who should be in your team. Check their availability for the period of the project. Analyse whether they have the skills required to enable them to carry out their role. If not, ensure they receive the right training.
5. Identify those who are affected and 'impacted' by the project – the stakeholders. This should be an in-depth analysis, which needs updating regularly.

6. Hold a kick-off meeting (start-up workshop) with key stakeholders, the sponsor and the team. Use the meeting to help develop the PID. Identify risks and generally plan the project. If appropriate, hold new meetings at the start of a new stage.
7. Ensure you review the project during the 'defining your project' stage – involve your project sponsor or senior manager in this process. Remember to check progress against the business case.

Delivery planning

During the delivery planning stage you should create a Work Breakdown Structure (WBS) for the project; an example is shown in Figure 5.2. A WBS is a key element you will need to develop in your plan. It lists all of the activities you will have to undertake to deliver the project. Post-it notes can be a great help in developing this. Group tasks under different headings once you have a list, as this will enable you to identify the chunks of work that need to be delivered.

Identify dependencies (or predecessors) of all activities. This will let you put together the Gantt (a bar chart) and milestone charts. The layout of these charts has the list of activities on the left hand side of the page, the timescale across the top in any units that you want – days, weeks, months, according to the duration of the project. The bars that you create indicate the length of time that an activity is estimated to take. It is a good idea to have 'empty' bars that can then be filled in as you complete a task, or use different colours to indicate when an activity is finished.

Ensure you write everything down otherwise you are trying to carry potentially hundreds of options in your head. Estimating how long each activity will take might sound pretty straightforward, but in reality people are notoriously bad at this. So, if you estimate a task will take three days, consider how confident you are that you can deliver in three days by using a percentage measure – for

Work Breakdown Structure (WBS) Dictionary Form

Project: _____   WBS Element Number: _____

WBS Name: _____   Parent WBS Number: _____

Date: _____

Revision Date:
Revision Reason:

_____

Description:

_____

_____

_____

_____

Required Effort:

_____

_____

_____

Assumptions:

_____

_____

_____

Parameters:

_____

_____

_____

WBS Cost Elements:

_____

_____

Figure 5.2   WBS form

example, I'm only 40 per cent certain I can deliver in three days. You should be aiming for 80 per cent. If you do not achieve 80 per cent, recalculate. Then:

1. Identify the critical path for the project. This identifies those activities which have to be completed by the due date in order to complete the project on time.
2. Communicate, communicate, communicate! Delivering a project effectively means you need to spend time communicating with a wide range of individuals. Build a communication plan and review it regularly and include it in your Gantt chart. Are you involved in a major change project? If you are, think through the implications of this for key stakeholders and how you may need to influence and communicate with them.
3. Conduct a risk assessment – carry out a full risk analysis and document it in a risk register. Regularly review each risk to ensure you are managing them, rather than them managing you. Appoint a person to manage each risk.
4. Review the GANTT chart. You can use the milestone dates to check that the project is where it should be. Review whether activities have been delivered against the milestone dates and take a look forward at what needs to be achieved to deliver the next milestone.

Evaluate your project

Have a clear project management monitoring and reviewing process – agreed by senior managers, the project sponsor and the project board, if you have one. Be aware early in the project what will be monitored, how monitoring will be carried out and the frequency. Keep accurate records of your project, not only for audit purposes but also to ensure you have documents that enable you to monitor changes. Use a Planned vs Actual form. It is easy to create – it allows you to monitor how you are progressing with specific tasks in terms of time and money. Link these forms into milestone reviews.

Identify with your sponsor the type of control that is needed – loose or tight or a variation of these; eg tight at the start, loose in the middle, tight at the end. Ensure the system you develop reflects the type of control intended. Have an agreed system for monitoring and approving changes. Use change control forms and obtain formal sign-off (agreement) by the project sponsor before actioning a change. Look for the impact of the change on the project scope as well as the 'key driver' – quality, cost and time. Make it clear to everyone that honest reporting against specific deliverables, milestones, or a critical path activity is essential. If you do not have honest reporting, imagine the consequences.

During this stage you need to see whether you are still delivering the original project benefits when reviewing your project. If not, consider re-scoping or, if appropriate, abandoning the project. Do not be afraid of abandoning a project. Better to stop now than waste valuable time, money and resources working on something no longer required. If you close a project early, hold a project review meeting to identify learning.

Then (hold on to your hats, this is a big stage!):

1. Appoint someone to be responsible for project quality, especially in larger projects. Review quality formally with the client at agreed milestone dates.
2. Make certain you have agreed who can sanction changes in the absence of your project sponsor. If you haven't agreed this, what will you do in their absence?
3. Set a time limit for project meetings to review progress. Have an agenda with times against each item and summarise after each item at the end of the meeting. Produce action points against each item on the agenda and circulate within 24 hours of the meeting. Use these action points to help in the creation of your next agenda.
4. Review the items on the critical path, checking they are on schedule. Review risks, review your stakeholders and

your communication plans and whether you are still on track to deliver on time, to budget and to the required quality standard.

5. Set a tolerance figure and monitor, eg a tolerance figure of ±5 per cent means that as long as you are within the 5 per cent limit, you do not have to formally report. If you exceed the 5 per cent limit (cost or time) then you need to report this to the agreed person – probably your project sponsor.

6. Report progress against an end of a stage – are you on schedule? Review time, cost or quality. Ensure that if something is off schedule the person responsible for delivering it suggests ways to bring it back on time, within budget, or to hit the right quality standard.

7. Documentation: develop an issues log to record items that may be causing concern. Review at your project meetings. Produce one-page reports highlighting key issues. Agree with the project sponsor the areas to include before writing a report. Use a series of templates to support the monitoring process, eg milestone reporting, change control log and planned vs actual. Apply traffic lights to illustrate how you are progressing – red, amber and green. Use these in conjunction with milestone reports.

Close down and review

Agree well in advance a date to hold a post-project review meeting. Put this onto the Gantt chart. Invite key stakeholders, the sponsor and the project team to the meeting. If the date is in their diary well in advance it should make it easier for them to attend.

Focus your meeting on learning – identifying what you can use on the next project. Share the learning with others in the organisation. Check whether you have delivered the original project objectives and benefits and not gone out of scope. Make sure that you have delivered against budget, quality requirements and the end deadline. Understand how well you managed risks and your key stakeholders. Use questionnaires to obtain feedback. Then:

1. Prepare a list of any unfinished items. Identify who will complete these after the project and circulate to any stakeholders.
2. Hand over the project formally to another group (it is now their day job) – if appropriate. You may need to build this into the project plan and involve them early in the plan and at different stages throughout the project.
3. Write an end of project report and circulate. Identify in the report key learning points.
4. Close the project formally. Inform others you have done this and who is now responsible for dealing with day-to-day issues.

Finally, celebrate success with your team! Recognise achievement: there is nothing more motivating.

Hint

Discover how project management software can help. You will still need to develop the business case, produce a project definition alongside planning what will go into the software. Many project managers use simple Excel spreadsheets or charts in Word to help deliver their project.

Phew! With all the detail I have given you, good luck with keeping your next project on track, bringing it in on time, and within budget.

Checklist for action

- Regularly review the methods you use for disseminating information – getting communication through to the team, and up to your superiors. Are you using the correct communication methodology and channels in each instance, or does something need to change?
- When running formal meetings make sure AOB (Any Other Business) is taken off the agenda!
- Build a 'web of influence' around you. Create 'political alliances' with others who can help you fight your corner.
- Remember during your next project that project management is not just a methodology. You have got to get people on your side to achieve your objectives.

6

Taking over as manager of an established team

Introduction

Suppose you have been asked to take over an existing team. In this chapter we are going to look at the considerations you need to take into account that wouldn't be the case if you were setting up a team from scratch.

First we will look at the different circumstances in which you might be taking over the team. Are you taking over because someone is moving on to a more senior role, or has your predecessor been fired? Is the team high performing, average, or under-performing? We will then look at your relationship with your team and how you should go about building trust and respect, and finally the timeline and activities you should undertake to enhance the performance of your team.

In what circumstances are you taking over the team?

If you are an external hire you will need to be briefed in detail about the overall strategy of the organisation and how your team fits into the big picture. As an internal hire you will already be up to speed on organisational strategy. There is a good chance that people will know who you are – your reputation will go before you. Whether this is good or bad news only time will tell!

There are two scenarios to consider: was your predecessor sacked or moved sideways because of underperformance of the team, or is the current post holder going to be promoted and be your boss? If your predecessor was sacked, you will have been brought in to problem solve and turn the team's performance around. Changes can be made far more overtly and implemented immediately. In fact, it is advantageous to make changes relatively early on to get over the resistance you might encounter with your direct reports saying: 'It has always been done this way.' You have to bear in mind as well that if a team leader/manager has been fired due to underperformance of the team, those in the team might be feeling insecure: 'Is my job on the line as well?' Taking a firm hand and bringing in changes sooner rather than later should assure them, and create a more positive attitude in the team.

If, however, the current post holder is going to be promoted and be your boss you should initially tread more cautiously regarding changes that you might want to make to the running of the team. You should assess what is working well – don't throw the baby out with the bath water. If in your view something needs to change, take time to reflect. (Let's face it, your manager would have hardly been promoted if the team was under-performing!) Keep the strategy as it is and then gradually, over a six-month to one-year period, bring in the changes that are required.

It is also important to establish your authority as the new manager/team leader. You must have 100 per cent backing from the person you report to. If your manager was previously in post it could be a temptation for members of the team to keep going back to him or her for guidance, for example during a problem-solving activity. This could undermine your authority. You don't want to live in the shadow of your predecessor. It is up to you to make the distinction very clear to all that you are now the person members of the team come to for guidance should they require help.

Your relationship with the team and stakeholders

The style of management that you adopt when you are joining an existing team will usually differ initially from the style of management that you would use when setting up a team from scratch. When joining an existing team you need to show your power more overtly, and act in a more authoritative manner to start off with, until you see the exact 'lie of the land'. If you find that the team is performing well, you can allow them to self-manage quite quickly and use a facilitative style of leadership on an ongoing basis. If the team is failing you need to have a tighter hold on the reins in order to analyse why the team is under-performing.

You should be mindful of the fact that the team may have agreed between themselves their approach to dealing with you before you joined. There is nothing you can do about this upfront, but your first role is to demonstrate that you are an active listener, and someone who does what they say. This is the first step in building trust.

You have got to be able to communicate realistically as well. This means being very precise with your language, objectives, measures and stakeholder benefits. You need to demonstrate your business acumen, so that those in the team can judge for themselves why you have been asked to head up the team. Bear in mind there could be a person/people in the team that considered themselves suitable for the role, and they have been overlooked for the post you have taken on.

The team or company's key clients are obviously of importance. You have to establish a working relationship with these decision makers as soon as possible. The aim is to ensure that key clients have a relationship with the organisation rather than with the individual.

You should get yourself up to speed with all the systems, processes and procedures, and be wary that certain members of the team might want to hide information from you, for their own purposes – information is power. I have experienced this when joining teams. In one instance I was to take over the running of the organisation's main blue chip account, including other roles and responsibilities. The outgoing account manager for this major account only gave me the barest operational details, and certainly no information about recent problems that had occurred during programmes we had run for this client. In another instance, when I became director of a business unit in the education sector, one of the client managers in the department told me that she did not have a database of her current or past clients, when in reality she had a database of several hundred. So make sure that all databases are centralised and not on individuals' PCs or laptops.

Teams need a plan to give them a sense of direction and purpose. Your plan should be much more than a schedule of near-term activities. It has to fully embrace the meaning and context of the work you and your team do, identify the forces shaping your environment and describe the future you want and the strategies for creating it.

Hints

Don'ts
Don't try to establish a personal friendship with members of your team too soon in the working relationship. Keep it friendly but professional.

Don't make sweeping changes to protocol, processes or procedures too soon when joining the team. You need time to understand the rationale behind all of these activities, and how they link in with other parts of the organisation.

Bear in mind that, whether you like it or not, there are 'sacred cows' in any organisation that can't be changed. Make yourself aware of these, fight your corner if you think your case is strong, but don't be dispirited if your recommendations aren't adopted. This is not being defeatist, just pragmatic.

Don't presuppose that there are standards or agreements in place on quality, quantity, budgetary spend and timing. Gain an understanding of the workflow and brainstorm with your team to establish these standards.

Don't wait for key decision makers throughout the organisation to come to you. Be proactive. Set up meetings with stakeholders as soon as feasible.

Timelines for progress

So let's look at the tangible steps you can take when you have been told you are to join and manage an existing team.

Step 1 (first two weeks)

Prior to joining the team you need to know what power you have. Meet with your manager and agree the power parameters of your role; what your responsibilities are (and are not) and clarify your objectives and measures and how often you will be evaluated. Of course, this applies when starting a new team from scratch. The difference when taking over an established team is to understand if there are issues that have resulted in the team under-performing.

You also need to establish what is important to your manager and what he or she expects from you in your new role. Your direct manager is crucial, since he or she can stall or ruin your future career prospects and you want to know what they expect from you. You have been selected for this role for a reason. You should ask your manager to explain why you were selected, and what he or she requires you to accomplish and by when. If you do not do this, you might not grasp key issues from your most important stakeholder. You have been warned. You must ensure you know how you will be measured. Agree these measures in writing to ensure you have not been set up to fail.

Once you have done this you must turn your attention to your team members. Have one-to-one meetings with each team member, and do a mini appraisal – see if you have winners or under-performers. (If you were setting up a team from scratch, you would usually have more choice about who you recruit and induct.) Your first task is to *listen* to them:

- **Who are they?**
- **How long have they been in position?**
- **What do they actually do?**
- **How closely does what they do align with team objectives and required outputs?**
- **How do they feel about having a new manager?**
- **What do they expect now and in the medium term?**
- **(If they are a long-established team) how honest will they be with you?**
- **What's working well in the way the team performs?**
- **What's not working well and why?**
- **How motivated is the team?**
- **Who, in the team, is performing and who is not?**
- **How clearly defined is the team mission and vision?**
- **How do internal/external customers respond to the team?**
- **What do team members expect from their (new) manager?**

Once the above is complete you must now turn your attention to your team's stakeholders (colleagues, internal/external clients/ suppliers). Your first task is to *listen* to them too:

- **Who are they?**
- **What do they expect from your team/team members?**
- **What is the actual level of service they receive?**
- **To what degree does the team add value to stakeholders?**
- **What do stakeholders expect from the new team manager?**
- **What do they expect now and in the medium term?**
- **What's working well in the way the team performs?**
- **What's not working well and why?**
- **Who, in the team, is performing and who is not?**
- **How motivated are they working with the team?**
- **How often should you talk to stakeholders?**

Do not agree or disagree with what you hear. Take notes and simply tell those you meet when you will get back to them. You must meet this deadline.

> ## Tip
> One of the first things you should say to a member of the team is: 'How can I help you?'

Step 2 (first four weeks)

Invite your entire team to a meeting and communicate to them the messages you have heard from your discussions. Ask the team for their proposals to implement improvements and create an action plan with due dates and those responsible to address stakeholder issues. Concentrate on those things that have immediate impact and get stakeholders talking positively about you and your team.

Step 3 (first six weeks)

Since your team is an established one your next task is to 're-recruit' them under your mentorship:

- **Are there team members who want to leave?**
- **Are there team members you want to keep (no matter what)?**
- **Have you identified any skills or competency gaps?**
- **Is there any coaching or training required?**

Do all you can to keep your key people. They can be the cornerstones of your team effort, so don't take them for granted. Make them feel important. In turn, invest the same time and effort in creating the overall team that you would in recruiting a new employee. Try to capture people's spirit. Put some fire into their feeling about the work in hand. Ensure they're on board *emotionally*. Successful teamwork depends heavily on your ability to stabilise and energise the group.

Having reviewed the skills and competencies of the members of the team, are there any hidden talents that need to be utilised? If there are weak players that have to stay, give them the guidance and coaching they might need, but don't let this dominate your working day. You need to build on positive energy and attitude in the team. If the weak players' performance/attitude does not improve, you must position them where they will hurt the team least.

If development is required, will coaching be sufficient or are internal learning resources available? For example, are in-house programmes run regularly, are there distance learning or computer based materials that might be used? Is there a library for self-study? Might public courses run by an external supplier be the best option? Will 'sitting with Nelly' suffice (on the job training)?

Draw up an appropriate training and development plan in collaboration with those that require assistance.

If you envisage job descriptions are to be changed, check with your HR department on any grading implications. Ensure you have the budget to cover these changes. Check out the protocol you have to go through if you wish to put someone through a disciplinary procedure. Your HR department will be able to supply you with this information.

Decide what style of team you want to create. What are they ready for? How far do you want to take them down the self-managed route?

Make sure that the decision-making process is working effectively. Do members of the team have the appropriate level of authority to act? If not, redress the balance.

Ensure everyone in the team has agreed performance standards and knows how and when they will be monitored.

Step 4 (first 2 months)

The way you behave will endorse the fact that you are a transformational manager. The moulding of the team's culture must be clearly and visibly led by you. You should become a personal walking advertisement and use example behaviour to reinforce the changes you wish to implement.

Show that the team's values equate with 'winners' feelings. Your team are not going to be winners unless they are more efficient and innovative in the eyes of your stakeholders. You need to re-clarify why the team exists as a team (the mission), and communicate where they are going (the vision). In turn you should agree objectives for each person based on any changes that you might be implementing.

Step 5 (keeping the momentum going)

In line with what characterises a successful team that we have explored in earlier chapters, it can be useful to extend and adapt Belbin's team roles into a questioning approach, as follows.

In our team activities, are we:

- **Adopting a more resilient approach to challenges and obstacles?**
- **Careful to look for omissions, mistakes and errors and ensuring they do not occur again?**
- **Accessing sufficient specialist skills?**
- **Clarifying and promoting decision taking and delegating appropriately?**
- **Looking at options and judging well?**
- **Listening to each other and dealing with interpersonal conflict?**
- **Producing imaginative and creative solutions?**
- **Exploring opportunities and developing both internal and external contacts?**
- **Producing the means for practical implementation?**

In this list the names of team roles have been eliminated and the description of the contribution has been reframed as a question. It is a useful tool and in my experience it generates a level of discussion and self-examination that enables the team to focus on how they might improve their processes, or possibly reassure themselves that they are on track and doing the right things.

Problem busting

There are a myriad of different scenarios that you might encounter when taking over an existing team. Let's look at three typical scenarios you might experience:

1. Team members being in different age categories with different skill sets and career (or retirement) aspirations.

2. A project failing even though it appears everyone is on board at the start of the project.
3. Lack of inspiring team purpose or clarity with tangible business benefits in a language all stakeholders understand.

Scenario 1

Team members being in different age categories with different skills sets and career (or retirement) aspirations.

Let's take an example of your taking over a team for a year-long project that needs to be re-energised and changed to achieve the defined outcome.

Several members of the team are in their 20s and 30s. This age category is known as 'Generation Y' and is at ease with multimedia technology. There is also someone in the team in his/her late 40s, in the age category known as 'Generation X'. He/she is good at the 'technical' side of the work; for example he/she is very knowledgeable about products and procedures and has been with the company for 20 years. However, he/she is not at ease with accessing information from a PC, and you can see from the word go that he/she is not going to cooperate and do his/her fair share of the workload. He/she has turned off and is coasting towards retirement. In addition, he/she has seen lots of these change initiatives before. He/she maintains a laissez-faire approach, expecting any changes you introduce to fail. He/she says little either for or against the project.

So what does this mean in terms of managing, coaching and development with each generation? In my experience Generation Y will usually consider that they are aware of the communication ethos – even that they are good communicators. What they need is to have the capacity to be self-critical and self-analytical rather than simply communicating in multimedia formats. They also need more work experience to help them develop decision-making skills. Technology is not the total solution to everything! They need to act and behave in accordance with the demands of stakeholders in a language they, the stakeholders, understand.

For the Generation X member of the team, you must ensure that what he/she agrees to do is done, and on time. He/she may use excuses. Your role is to ensure when he/she says 'yes' you *know* that he/she is committed to taking action. First, he/she needs to be aware of the impact his/her lack of action will have on the project and you simply must embarrass him/her into taking action. You will need to take a more hands-on role to start off with by defining and agreeing his/her input to the project and the timing for each segment of activity that he/she is undertaking. Meet and audit his/her workload and don't allow slippage. As his/her performance improves, gradually ease him/her into the rest of the group who are self-managing their workload. Keep a vigilant eye until you are assured that he/she is pulling his/her weight in the team, and not going to slip back to his/her bad old ways.

As a postscript, don't disregard the Generation X person as being out of touch simply because he/she is less proficient with technology. He/she is likely to have in-depth business and organisational knowledge and personal contacts that will help you to get things done in unorthodox and invaluable ways for the longer term greater good of the project and/or for the day-to-day functioning of the team.

Scenario 2

A project failing even though it appears everyone is on board at the start of the project.

CASE STUDY   Why things can go wrong with a project

The main board of a leading UK consultancy group decided as part of their strategic plan to expand the company's public courses unit, in order to generate more leads for new business to the various operating departments. This is a classic ploy in consultancy groups. Public courses are run to attract delegates to use the services of the organisation in one capacity, with a view to lead generation for the selling of other services, such as research, consultancy or in-house training.

A business development director was hired to manage this unit. One of the board of directors was to be her sponsor. When she took over the Short Course Unit there were a limited number of programmes that were offered. She was told it was important to use staff within the organisation, not bring in external consultants. She was also advised to use staff who had particular specialised knowledge, be this in finance, law, or technology or any specialism that the consultancy group wanted to promote at any point in time to enhance their reputation in the marketplace.

So far so good. She took over a small team who were undertaking the operational activities for running the existing programmes, and set about liaising with consultants in the various departments, asking them if they could allocate two or three days (according to the topic) to deliver public courses for her unit. If they agreed, the consultant put together a course outline that went into the new public course brochure that was being produced. An agreed internal cross-charge was allocated for the time taken by the consultant to deliver the programmes. The scheduling of dates for this booking was of necessity several months in advance as the brochure was published at the beginning of each year.

Bookings started to come in for the new programmes, and the business development director could see that even though she might have to run the programmes at break-even to start off with, once word got around about the new programmes she had every opportunity to make the business unit viable. But horror of horrors happened. As the date of a course approached more often than not the consultant who was allocated to deliver the session would call to say that he or she could no longer deliver the two- or three-day programme, as an in-house client had booked them for a several week assignment. She had to cancel delegates booked on the course, and this gave potential purchasers a negative rather than a positive overall perception of the organisation.

The funds that had been allocated for this new venture only covered the costs of running the unit for two years and by year two, even though certain courses went ahead and were well attended, the unit was running at a substantial deficit. As a result, the Short Course Unit was closed down.

Exercise

Task

With the information provided in the case study, answer these questions:

- What went wrong with this assignment, which apparently had the blessing of the main board?
- Why didn't consultants make the public training programmes a firm non-negotiable booking?
- What should have been in place to ensure that the public programmes acted as a good PR tool for the organisation, rather than a negative experience?

Response

One of the main issues is that the two- or three-day public course delivery was a 'nice to have' activity for the consultants who elected to put forward a new programme for the public course calendar. It was not an essential part of their job description or linked into their performance measures. The term 'nice to have' can also apply to mentoring or coaching in an organisation. If it is not built into the agreed objectives at performance review time, there is no obligation on the member of staff to take on these additional activities.

Why did her sponsor not have more clout at board level? Who knows? There could be a variety of reasons. Perhaps he did not present the issues the Short Courses Unit was experiencing in a convincing enough manner. Or it could have been a conflict of interest for the other heads of departments on the board. Their in-house client work would generate more revenue for their departments than the two- or three-day internal cross-charge fee they would receive from the Short Courses Unit.

Thirdly, it was the role of the business development director to mitigate risk wherever she could. She should have put a contract/Project Charter in place with the individual consultants who were delivering the programmes to say that if they were not in a position to deliver their session they could find another consultant with similar skill sets to run the programme on their behalf.

If the sponsor had flagged the problem soon enough at board level he could have got agreement that if Plan A – using a consultant from a department – turned out to not be feasible, then the business development director would have the right to use an external consultant. This would mean she could have had as an additional contingency plan a list of external suppliers she could call on if needs must.

Here is an example of what a Project Charter might contain.

Computing Project

We have assigned Peter Smith to be the project manager for the Computing Project. This project is an important project for ABC Research/XYZ Corporation. When complete, the project will significantly increase ABC/XYZ's productivity and quality measures by providing instant and universal access to the company's data and programs.

As project manager, Peter Smith is responsible for working with your team to develop a project plan that describes the objectives, deliverables and implementation plan for the project. He will work with functional managers at ABC Research and XYZ Corporation to assign the appropriate resources to the project. He will also coordinate with you and other managers at XYZ Corporation to identify the resources needed from your company.

He will execute the project plan, monitor progress and performance, and take corrective action if necessary. He will communicate assignments to functional managers and the members of the project team. For the duration of the project, Peter Smith will prepare and present status reports every two weeks to the ABC Research/XYZ Corporation project steering committee.

To ensure the success of the project, Peter Smith has the authority to manage the project, assign resources and make financial commitments on behalf of ABC Research. His authority for the Computing Project specifically includes:

- **Communicating directly with XYZ Corporation regarding the project.**
- **Communicating directly with the ABC Research management team regarding the project.**
- **Making financial decisions relating to the project, including procurement, expenditures and authorising payments.**
- **Delegating authority and responsibilities to resources with the approval of the resources' functional managers.**
- **Negotiating with functional managers and customer contacts for resources.**
- **Requesting assistance from any member of the steering committee to help resolve issues that arise.**

I have the utmost confidence in Peter Smith and ask that you support him in achieving the objectives of this project. If you have any questions about his authority or responsibilities, please contact me.

Regards,

Anthony Spencer,
Sponsor for the Computing Project

As you can see from the above:

- **The first paragraph states the benefit for both the organisations that are going to be involved in this project.**
- **The next paragraph states the objectives of the project and staff that are to be involved.**
- **The third paragraph specifies how progress is to be communicated, and to whom.**
- **Following this, the authority for managing the project is specified in detail.**
- **The final paragraph asks for their support in achieving the project and, if there are any generic questions, who to contact.**

Scenario 3

Lack of inspiring team purpose or clarity with tangible business benefits in a language all stakeholders understand.

I was undertaking a team-building assignment within a blue chip IT organisation in the UK. When I talked to each member of the team during the research phase, there seemed to be a lack of clarity about what they were to achieve during a particular project. Any communication that had come from the top team did not seem particularly relevant to them, and was not put in language that they could understand. 'There's one of those "management-speak" memos again' was the typical comment in the team.

What was going wrong? The language both parties used. Senior management spoke in terms of profit, revenue and resource management. Team members spoke in terms of day-to-day activities that helped them to deliver intermediate objectives on the way to delivering team goals.

The key responsibility of the team leader is to manage the communication between stakeholders to ensure that everyone involved understands the meaning, ie the benefits delivered by the team help all involved to meet their personal objectives. The team leader's job is to translate communication to ensure it is presented in a language relevant to each hierarchical level so that it is immediately understood by that level. If they don't do this they will get blamed by stakeholders.

Checklist for action

- If a team is under-performing ensure that you are not only getting a true picture of the issues but also the full backing of your manager for any changes you want to make.
- When first meeting with your stakeholders, remember you have two ears and one mouth. Use them in that ratio.
- Be a walking advertisement of the behaviour you expect from others. Remember your ultimate aim is to realign the team's identity with your leadership style.
- Ensure all written communication uses wording that your team can understand and relates to their jobs.
- Mitigate risk wherever you can. If the situation warrants it, create a Project Charter to ensure comprehensive understanding for all parties concerned.

7

Problems in the team

Introduction

Teams are a fact of life. Your family is (or should be) a team. Most of us never quite realise when we are happy with our family until things go wrong. Then our frustration builds. Unfortunately, most of us are untrained so we cannot put into words why we feel the way we do and come up with a practical solution to address the situation. All we know is that it isn't working well. It's exactly the same with teams.

There can be small niggles, things that irritate others and stop the team working as effectively as it should. Problems can result in work not being delegated as it should be. What else? Ah yes, sometimes I have seen teams working on problem-solving activities and they haven't got to the real cause of the problem to start off with! Innovation and creativity can be noticeably absent in the average team (apart from teams that are staffed with people from a creative or innovative background). Getting people to think more expansively about their work, or lateral thinking about how to solve a problem, should be part of their everyday activities. But how do you shake people out of inertia and get them to do this?

All of these, what I describe as 'work-based problem' areas, will be explored in the first part of the chapter. The second part will look at what I call 'people problems'.

Work-based problems

Work-based problems are apparent when there are issues with the task in hand. It can appear at times that everyone is spinning on his or her heels and nothing is being accomplished. It could be that the team does not understand the common goal they should be achieving, and are all working on different bits and pieces of the project without any cohesion.

As the team leader you need to be sure that you have the right mix and complement of skills to achieve the task in hand, and that the correct communication channels with other stakeholders are in place. You also need to make sure people have the right resources available to undertake the task.

So let's get down to specific problems now and investigate them in more detail.

Problem 1

There can be an imbalance of workload. One person seems to be overloaded with work and does not trust others to help because he or she feels it's quicker to do things him or herself than it would be explaining the process to someone else. (Could this be you?)

Way forward

Let's take this as being you the team leader finding yourself overwhelmed with your workload and wanting to pass work on to those in your team. What do you need to do first?

Go through your workload and categorise the activities you need to undertake and work out with steely-eyed vision what is of high importance and high urgency. This is where your focus needs to be at any one time. Now don't tell me that *everything* is of high importance and high urgency – our working lives aren't like that! You clearly have to keep part of your workload just for you, as it is part of your roles and responsibilities. For example, you are responsible for creating the vision, overall planning, motivation and performance management of the team. You can't delegate these – and let's face it, it's no mean task to keep all of these elements of your work in place. But when it comes down to things like creating a new brochure, finding a new distributor for your products, researching, or upgrading the IT system, you can easily pass these activities on to others. You might enjoy doing some of these things, but tough luck, you can't do everything! So:

1. List your responsibilities. Then select those that you can delegate to others.
2. For each responsibility choose who in your team can do the job already or who can be trained.
3. Ensure both of you understand what's involved by setting concrete (what it is, when exactly and contain a figure) guidelines.
4. Give clear guidance on the results you expect and when you expect them.
5. Encourage questions. Let him or her choose the route or methods and means so that he or she 'feels' responsible for the results.
6. Let the person know what HR, financial or other resources are available to him or her.
7. Specify how and when you will evaluate his or her performance.
8. Agree how achievement of the results will be rewarded. A 'reward' can be as simple as letting the person concerned move on to a particular assignment he or she has expressed interest in. Or, if the work has been a substantial part of his or her workload for the year, you will have agreed with him or her beforehand how the outcome will be assessed and rewarded at appraisal time.

When a team leader delegates, the team member becomes responsible for doing that task. He or she is given the authority to make decisions in connection with that task, and should be allowed to get on with the job without interference. If you are unsure of his or her abilities, ask team members to bring you their proposals *before* they implement them. This way you can stop mistakes being made and coach team members through the delegation process. It also gives you an opportunity to praise.

Delegation means giving the person the authority to do a job and making him or her accountable to you for the results. However, the act of delegation is not abdication and, although a team leader gives a member of the team the authority to perform within agreed limits, you are still ultimately responsible for the actions of this person. In other words, you 'carry the can' if things go wrong. You can delegate responsibility and authority, but you keep accountability.

If someone in your team needs to delegate to another person in the team you should make sure they go through the process above. Instil in them the importance of accountability. You don't want to get 53 messages of blame from them as to why outcomes have not been achieved.

Problem 2

Problem solving as a team can often falter because the root of the problem has not been identified properly.

Way forward

First, you need to consider whether you have defined your problem correctly. What questions have you asked? What questions should you have asked? For example, if you've been asking: 'Why aren't people buying our product/service?', try asking: 'Why *are* people buying our product/service?' or, 'Why aren't people who do buy from us buying more often?' or ,'Why are people buying from our competitor(s)?

Different questions will prompt different answers and so encourage different solutions. This process is called the 'Six honest serving men' method (Parnes *et al*, 1977). The six honest men are the words: *who, what, where, when, why* and *how*. The technique provides a framework for systematic information gathering; see Table 7.1. The information gathered often provides new perspectives on the issue being addressed, which in turn can lead to a redefinition of the problem.

Table 7.1 The 'six honest men' technique

Step	Process
A	State the problem in the format: 'In what ways might ...? *(IWWM)*
B	With regard to the problem, generate separate lists of the six questions: *Who, What, Where, When, Why and How* Write down the responses.
C	Examine the responses and use them to generate redefinitions of the problem.
D	Write down any redefinitions identified.
E	Select the redefinition that seems to reflect the issue most closely and work on it.

Another good tip is to ensure an accurate problem statement is made. So:

- **State the problem narrowly enough so the team can handle it.**
- **Make it a statement not a question.**
- **Be detailed, not too generous.**
- **Avoid doing the 'blame game' on any person or the cause.**

- As I have mentioned many times when I use the word 'concrete', use tangible and measurable qualities or quantities when you can.

Exercise

Take a look at these problem statements and see if you can determine what is wrong with them:

1. We don't have enough space for all the meetings we have to hold.
2. We could improve our productivity if we had air-conditioning.
3. The number of errors on the packaging production line is 0.65 per 1,000.
4. We get customer complaints about the phones not being answered between 1.00 pm and 2.00 pm.

How could these statements have been improved and made more tangible and measurable?

Answer:

1. This is too general and not measurable. A better statement would have been: 'In October 2011 we had to cancel six meetings because the five rooms allocated to our sales department were all occupied.'
2. This includes a solution in the statement, but it may not be the only solution. A better statement would have been: 'Productivity decreased by 15 per cent in the distribution unit between 1 April and 31 August 2011.'
3. Needless to say this is too woolly. To be effective it should have stated the total number of errors and over what time period the measurement was taken.
4. Well this is a start. But if you really want a problem statement that can be used to work on, it should have been much more

specific. It should have spelt out how many customers and how many calls; for example 'We have received seven complaints from our key customer, the xyz client saying between 1 and 31 October 2011 they did not get through to the customer services department between 1.00 pm and 2.00 pm.'

Problem 3

People don't seem to want to go the extra mile and consider different approaches during continuous improvement brainstorming sessions. There are no breakthrough ideas. In turn, when you get together to think about new products or services to offer to the market, there is a distinct lack of creative thinking in the team.

Way forward

These days, there's hardly a mission statement that doesn't herald creativity and innovation, or a senior manager who doesn't laud it. And yet despite all of the attention that business creativity has won over the past few years, maddeningly little is known about day-to-day creativity and innovation in the workplace.

One of the team leader's roles is to ensure *everyone* in your team comes up with novel and useful ideas, on a regular basis. Almost all of the recent research on creativity shows that anyone with normal intelligence is capable of expanding their horizons and doing some degree of creative work. Creativity depends on a number of things: experience, including knowledge and technical skills; talent; an ability to think in new ways; and the capacity to push through uncreative dry spells.

Intrinsic motivation

Intrinsic motivation – where people are turned on by their work is an important factor in getting people to push boundaries. You will often find that high achievers fit into this category. They need to feel, first and foremost, that the results they achieve are not by luck, but are created by the effort they put into achieving a particular goal. This is not about people being super-athletes and going for the gold medal. Intrinsic motivation is about people who are 'turned on' by effort, control and mastery of whatever they are working on. People in IT developing software products, scientists in pharmaceutical organisations, designers and engineers often fit into this category.

But supposing you don't have any of these people in your team. How can the concept of intrinsic motivation be of significance? I strongly believe that people don't go to work to just chat and waste their time and do the minimal amount of work. People want the opportunity to really engage in what they are doing, and make as much progress as is possible. A working life is not just about money. In fact bonuses and pay-for-performance plans can be problematic when team members believe that every move they make is going to affect their compensation. In such situations they may become risk-averse (this did not apply to the bankers during the economic crash of 2008!) Of course, people need to feel that they're being compensated fairly. But research shows that people put far more value on a work environment where creativity is supported, valued and recognised. So this means it's critical for team leaders to match people to projects not only on the basis of their experience but also in terms of where their interests lie. People are most creative when they care about their work and they're stretching their abilities and skills. If the challenge is far beyond their skill level, they tend to get frustrated; if it's far below their skill level, they tend to get bored. As team leader you need to be aware of this and strike the right balance.

One of the things you have to bear in mind is that when people are pushing boundaries they may sometimes fail. Failure will often come before success. In fact, if you have not failed you have not lived! Here are three famous examples:

> They were turned down by the Decca recording company – 'We don't like your sound. Guitar music is on the way out.' (This was the case with the Beatles.)

> 'I have missed more than 9,000 shots in my career. I've lost almost 300 games. Twenty-six times I have been trusted to take the game's winning

shot and missed. I've failed over and over again in my life. And that is why I succeed.' (Michael Jordan, former top US basketball player)

'His teacher told him he was stupid to learn anything, and that he should use his pleasant personality to get on in life.' (Thomas Edison, leading US inventor)

Not everyone can be intrinsically motivated. So how do you get these people to start thinking laterally and discovering other ways to do things? To get free-flowing conversation going, use brainstorming techniques.

Brainstorming

There's little doubt that brainstorming is the most well known and used of all creative problem-solving techniques. The term 'brainstorm' comes from the idea of using the brain to storm a problem. Osborn (1953) is often credited with being the inventor of brainstorming. Osborn emphasised that it is important to make sure that the generation of ideas is kept separate from the evaluation of those ideas. You can use this process for tackling:

- **new concepts for products/services;**
- **managerial problems;**
- **improvements to processes and procedures;**
- **planning and trouble-shooting.**

Ideally a brainstorming group should be made up of people from as wide and varied a background as possible. They should have an interest in helping with the issue without being too closely involved with it. Ideally, they should participate in the session with a mind free from preconceived ideas – they should be as 'open' as possible. There is no such thing as a perfect group size, though between four and 15 people is often quoted. Try to avoid people who are excessively dominant or insecure in group situations.

If possible, explain the process of brainstorming in advance to those taking part so that as much time as possible is given to generating ideas during the actual session. You may have to

begin with a 'warm-up' session in the first instance anyway
– experimenting with the concept for a while before tackling
the real issue.

The basic rules of brainstorming are:

- **State the issue to be discussed in basic terms, with only
  one focal point.**
- **Do *not* find fault with, or *stop* to explore, any one idea.**
- **Remember that *any* idea is acceptable.**
- **Provide the support and encouragement necessary to
  free people from their inhibitions.**

When running a brainstorming session:

- **Criticism is not permitted – adverse judgement of ideas
  is forbidden – no one is allowed to criticise anyone
  else's ideas.**
- **Freewheeling is positively welcomed – the wilder the
  better! People are encouraged to say *whatever* comes
  into their mind – the more peculiar the idea the better.
  Having such freedom – to say anything and everything
  – helps to stimulate more and more ideas.**
- **Quantity is good! The greater the number of ideas
  generated the more likelihood there is of some/one
  of them being a winner.**
- **Combinations/improvements should be encouraged
  – people should suggest how ideas of others can be
  improved upon or how two ideas can be joined together
  to create an even better one.**

Buzz sessions are useful if lots of people are involved. Everyone
is made aware of the issue or problem and then the large group
is divided into smaller brainstorming groups. Each group, with
its own leader, brainstorms the issue in the conventional way.
At the end of the session, the group selects the best idea(s) and
the leader presents it/them to the other groups. The best ideas
from the whole group are carried forward.

Another proven, successful process for brainstorming is to take two flip charts and put at the top of one sheet of paper, Step A, and on the other sheet, Step B. Start on the Step A flip chart. Imagine for example, that you have been asked to lead an innovation group, to come up with some positive ideas to move your organisation forward. Begin by brainstorming as described above. Move on to the Step B flip chart and agree your evaluation criteria. For example these might be:

- **quality of service;**
- **innovation;**
- **organisational issues; and**
- **cost-effectiveness.**

You would then use these four criteria as a 'filter' for your ideas. If an idea scored high against all four criteria, the chances are that it would be worth taking forward. It is important to remember, though, that some ideas might only meet one of the criteria but could be so positive in that one area that they should also be taken forward.

I hope that these suggestions will help you get your team energised, open to new ideas, and more expansive and creative in their thinking. If you want to know more about creative thinking, check out Edward de Bono's *Six Thinking Hats: An essential approach to business management* (1999). It's an excellent guide for when you get stuck undertaking a brainstorming session, as it makes you consider approaches, how people might feel, and moves you on from always getting stuck in a negative mindset.

So, having looked at work-based problems in teams let's look now at people problems that might emerge.

People problems

People problems can be very diverse, and in a way even more challenging to handle than work-based problems. After all, you are going to have to tackle a person rather than a process or procedure that needs correcting.

What kind of problems might you encounter?

Problem 4

The team appears dysfunctional. There is a myriad of small things that don't seem to be working as they should do; people turn up late for work or meetings, dress code can be hit and miss, and certain people in the group have a rather abrasive way of speaking to others, or simply don't pull their weight in the team.

Way forward

It is not always big fundamental problems that can unsettle a team. You need to notice details. Watch out for small niggles that can rock the boat; they can become big problems. There could be issues about timekeeping – when people arrive in the morning and when they depart; how good people are at delivering documentation on time, or even how prompt people are at turning up for meetings. So time can be interpreted in many different ways. Other niggles could be dress code, or the language people use that could be interpreted as rude or off-hand, or their overall demeanour – their behaviour. If people are working in an open plan office, and these niggles remain unchecked, they can move from a small niggle to an out and out problem.

As the team leader, whether it is a new team forming or you moving into an existing team, it is vital that you establish your authority and manage expectations. This means setting out from the word go what you expect from them as members of the team, and confirming back to them, 'This is what you can expect from me.' There will be certain non-negotiable guidelines that need to be established by you, for instance company-wide policies on health and safety, dress code or the need for cover in the team or department throughout the day. Set down these givens, but then leave it up to the team to get together to create their own behavioural 'code of conduct'. You could get people saying to you:

'Well, this is written down in the Staff Handbook.' That is not enough. So often when people join an organisation they are given the Handbook, but nine times out of 10 they just check out pension systems, when they are going to get paid, and the amount of annual leave they can expect after they have been at the organisation over a period of years. Codes of conduct will certainly be there, but could appear either glaringly obvious, or be interpreted as too much like 'motherhood' statements.

This means there is a need for ownership with regard to how people relate to each other, the nature of service they should offer each other as internal customers, and timelines that are realistic according to the range of activities the team undertakes. Get the team to discuss, agree and write down their own code of conduct in language that has meaning to their circumstances and environment. This is about self-policing. It is a way of getting people to acknowledge a benchmark standard that has been agreed between all parties concerned. The general ground rules should be created as a basis for collaborating in a manner that enhances productivity, increases participation, and honours individual contributions, experience and knowledge.

Here are a few examples of what might be included:

- **The relationships between people in the team will be HOT (Honest, Open and Trustworthy).**
- **All inputs during discussions are equally valued.**
- **Discussions and disagreement will focus on the topic in hand, and not focus on people.**
- **Only one conversation will go on at a time (unless subgroups are working on a particular activity).**
- **At meetings we will all arrive on time. This will mean that the meeting will start and end on time.**
- **The team is responsible for the deliverables.**

The document that is created should be visible to all, so displayed in their work area. What you will probably find is that the group creates a set of standards that are far more challenging than you would have imposed on them should you have been an autocratic leader. Of course, if the team changes there needs to be flexibility in the document for changes to be discussed and agreed by the new combination of staff.

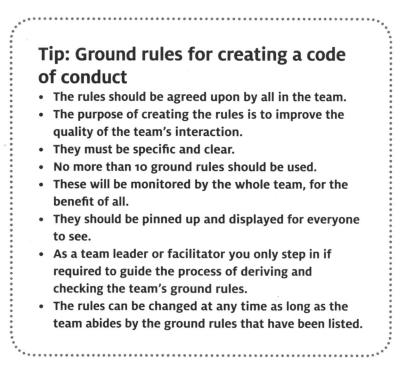

Tip: Ground rules for creating a code of conduct

- The rules should be agreed upon by all in the team.
- The purpose of creating the rules is to improve the quality of the team's interaction.
- They must be specific and clear.
- No more than 10 ground rules should be used.
- These will be monitored by the whole team, for the benefit of all.
- They should be pinned up and displayed for everyone to see.
- As a team leader or facilitator you only step in if required to guide the process of deriving and checking the team's ground rules.
- The rules can be changed at any time as long as the team abides by the ground rules that have been listed.

Problem 5

The team you have set up for a particular project are under-performing. Or it could be that an individual is not performing as you would want.

Way forward

Performance management is a key part of your job. Teams or an individual can underperform for a myriad of reasons. They might be disorganised, or not be able to prioritise. Equally, it could be a person in the team who is disruptive, or creates unnecessary conflict. One way or the other their behaviour is not acceptable. So what should you do?

Tip: Eight steps for handling underperformance during a project

These steps can apply to an individual or a team who is/are underperforming:

1. Focus on behaviour, not attitude.
2. Make a statement about what you have noticed/ observed, not what you feel. Make it as specific as possible.
3. Be silent – wait for a response.
4. Be focused on the present – right now. Talk about specific measurable goals.
5. Get them to come up with ideas as to how they can remedy their underperformance. Brainstorm ideas. Help them with priorities during a project.
6. Agree on the best approach. For example, 'Shall we have a weekly meeting to monitor progress?' What the meeting would look like – for example place/timing: 'Where is it best to meet, my office or yours?'
7. List all the tasks for the week, and jointly prioritise.
8. Monitor. Check in the agreed time frame – in the example in point 6, this would be on a weekly basis.

This process is not about you being right and them being wrong. It is about what sort of changes you want in performance. If you are dealing with either an individual or a team you need to gain agreement at the end of the project as to what they have learnt; for example, when they might need to come for advice or help, or what additional coaching/training they might need to ensure that the same underperformance does not happen again.

Tips: A few quick buzz ideas

Symptom 1: The team leader or a member of the team brings up an idea or concern, and the reaction from others is deadly silence. Perhaps their comment raises an awkward issue or it's simply that others need time to reflect. If this happens only occasionally, that's fine. What you want to ensure is that new ideas are always welcome and that stifling of ideas will not be tolerated.

A solution: Simply ask the team to consider their thoughts and prepare answers to your concerns for 5–10 minutes and then do a table round. Everyone should speak.

Symptom 2: Team members say 'yes' but nothing happens.

A solution: Check to see if the team is dominated by one or two members. Dominance by a few members can reduce participation by others. Any illusion of consensus may be false. Don't allow your team to be dragged down by a few powerful advocates. Without full consensus, commitment to decisions simply doesn't happen. These 'few' may deliberately block others' actions. If the team leader is perceived to be one of the draggers, this sends signals to others in the team that this is acceptable behaviour.

Symptom 3: Team members make statements like: 'He is ...' or, 'You are ...' Such statements can create enemies. When we agree with someone. they may become part of our clique; if we don't agree (and use the above statements) they may become an enemy. 'Personality' conflicts and sharp clashes of opinion can greatly affect team effectiveness.

The team leader's role is to stop such behaviour in its tracks.

A solution: Ensure team members use phrases like 'It seems to me ...' or, 'In my opinion ...' when talking about people. This way, their perceptions don't cloud their judgement.

Symptom 4: Several in the team are working on a project together but they seem to be muddling through without focus. Mistakes and errors are occurring on a daily basis during this initiative, and even though these errors have been highlighted during review meetings nothing seems to change. This can occur through 'groupthink'. This means members of a group feel invulnerable to error, rarely admit mistakes, and as a group they actively discourage disagreement.

A solution: Here, goals and objectives appear not to have been set in a precise enough manner. In addition, no one appears to be accountable for a particular part of the project. People are hiding themselves within the comfort of the group. They are not 'rocking the boat' by voicing their thoughts and ideas as to how the group should tackle the assignment. So goals, roles, and responsibilities need to be clearly defined. Objectives should be SMART (specific, measurable, achievable, realistic and timed). Goals, such as 'reduce cost by 10 per cent', 'improve quality', or 'get a better attitude' may be good to hear but meaningless until we agree on *what* costs, *what* measures of quality, and *what* behaviour constitutes an attitude.

With regard to the team roles, they need to be clearly defined so that they know what they should and should not do. Everyone in the team should also be really needed. There should not be passengers just along for the ride. In turn, the culture of the overall team should have instilled an attitude of thinking, questioning and arriving at a consensus on how to proceed, rather than just passive acceptance of the way forward.

Checklist for action

- Think through how tasks are delegated in your team. Do you personally need to pass over more work? Do you see a bottleneck of work piling up as a result of someone in your team not being able to cope with the workload, and not delegating to others? Take corrective action.
- Are you taking into account intrinsic motivation and making sure that people are undertaking projects they care about and that stretch their abilities and skills?
- Are you using diverse enough approaches to energise people's creative juices?
- If it does not already exist, get the team to create a 'Code of conduct' to define what they believe is acceptable and non-acceptable behaviour.
- For underperformance, focus on behaviour not attitude. Be specific and agree measurable goals.

Leading the virtual team

Introduction

Companies are increasingly moving towards setting up teams
that work remotely. Certain organisations might not even have
a permanent physical location. Instead, they maintain an
electronic presence in the marketplace. Physical facilities could
be leased or rented as required, and manufacturing if needed
could be outsourced. Technology developments and cost
reduction have been key drivers in these developments.

In this chapter we will explore the benefits and implications for
organisations working remotely, and how technology has helped
bring this about. Of course technology is not enough; we will
examine how interpersonal relationships and communication
between members of a virtual team are key to its survival and
success. We will then move on to getting the foundation stones
in place to make the team work, focusing on policies and
procedures, communication, information flow and the need
for trust and a sense of camaraderie. Finally, we will look at
predicting the virtual world of the future and the rise of the
neo-nomad.

The benefits and implications of working remotely

What are the benefits for companies working remotely? They include:

- **reduced operational costs;**
- **a global presence accessible from anywhere;**
- **24/7 opening hours;**
- **people being able to connect remotely regardless of time, space or organisational boundaries;**
- **localised skill shortages can be overcome.**

In addition, talented staff can be recruited from anywhere in the world. They don't have to relocate. On home soil, the demand for building and parking space can be reduced and therefore costs. Ecologically this is sound, reducing traffic congestion and pollution. In a nutshell, virtual teams offer more flexibility for staff and organisations.

However, working remotely has implications and costs for an organisation:

- **additional hardware, software and networks may need to be deployed;**
- **additional security may be required;**
- **staff need to be trained in the technology;**
- **those working remotely may need to work at non-traditional working times.**

For staff working remotely:

- **they can feel isolated and not part of the organisation;**
- **they have to discipline their time to ensure work-life balance;**
- **they could need help and guidance and not know where to find it.**

CASE STUDY   CareOne Services, Inc

CareOne Services is a debt collection agency based in Columbia, MD, in the United States. It currently has nearly 800 employees, and over two-thirds of these are part of a virtual workforce spread across the country. It initially created the virtual workplace programme in 2006 and found that being able to offer potential new staff the opportunity to work at home has been a plus factor during the recruitment process. A technology team coordinates communications between managers in headquarters and those working remotely. Members of the team also receive personal support and encouragement to achieve a healthy work-life balance.

Being able to offer this flexible work arrangement has helped the company to earn several workplace accolades, including being regularly named one of the Baltimore area's 'Best place to work' by both the *Baltimore Magazine* and the *Baltimore Business Journal*.

Technology to enable remote working

Let's start with looking at the enabling technology that has allowed remote working to happen.

Software designed for remote working, called 'groupware', is growing increasingly sophisticated (Lotus Notes and Exchange are two popular programmes). Getting groups of staff together from around the world has been enabled by desktop video conferencing, where all participants in a conversation can be viewed on the screen regardless of their geographic location. Audio teleconference links allow a team to work in real time so that they can come to an agreement about a tricky decision that needs to be made immediately. Websites and the intranet can store work schedules (who is working on what project at any one point in time), reference materials, graphics and flowcharts, or any key information that might be required for a particular assignment.

For day-to-day contact, e-mail is a given, as are traditional modes of contact such as the telephone, audio conferencing, voicemail and faxes. Across the whole organisation an electronic bulletin board allows anyone to post a question about changes that are happening, and hear from others in the organisation about what is going on from their point of view. An electronic suggestion box on a web page can provide a way for anyone in the organisation to make suggestions or come up with ideas for improvement. This can be done anonymously if the person posting the suggestions wishes it to be that way.

Remember, though: at the end of the day, technology doesn't make teams work. It allows good teams to function more effectively.

CASE STUDY   Severn Trent

It is interesting to see how this company have used technology to its advantage in making a relocation move go seamlessly for staff who are being relocated to a new site.

In the autumn 2010 the water company, Severn Trent needed to relocate 1,800 staff from 14 offices into a central office in Coventry. They used desktop virtualisation technology, fitting each desk in the new offices with a thin client machine that enables staff to work anywhere in the new building. Each machine can access any Severn Trent's employee's desktop and applications by streaming them from a central server. It has meant ultimately that staff can also work anywhere accessing their materials over the internet from outside the office.

The new office in Coventry has been designed to hold 1,500 staff even though there are 1,800 staff being relocated, which means that virtual teams are a given, offering flexibility and choice for both the company and employees.

(Heath, 2010)

Working with others in a virtual team

But is technology enough? How about interpersonal contact and communication? Does this go by the board for those working in virtual teams? What are some of the stumbling blocks that need to be overcome in this 'brave new world'?

When first taking over the role of team leader of a virtual team, you might think:

- **Will I ever be able to get my head around all this new technology?**
- **How can I coach or mentor in this environment?**
- **How can I monitor the performance of staff who are working on different continents?**
- **How can I build a sense of belonging to this team when people don't meet face-to-face?**
- **Can I trust those that report to me to do a good day's work?**

The management consultant Warren Bennis talks about trust being the 'emotional glue' that binds followers and leaders together. Charles Handy writes: 'If we are to enjoy the efficiencies and other benefits of the virtual organisation, we will have to rediscover how to run organisations based more on trust than on control. Virtuality requires trust to make it work. Technology on its own is not enough' (Handy, 1995). How true this is.

What fundamental skills do you need to manage a virtual team, and how do these skills differ from working with a 'normal' functional team?

Tips: Leadership skills for a virtual team

The first list of bullet points is the same as for a traditional team leader:

- The ability to align team initiatives with general organisational needs.
- Ensuring that the organisational values and objectives are understood and adhered to.
- The ability to access, analyse and manage data.
- Being able to manage, focusing on outcomes, results, schedules and budgets.
- Creating an environment built on trust and integrity.
- Being a good networker: gaining the support of internal and external customers.
- Disseminating information to the team and forwarding information to senior management in a timely manner.
- Striving for continuous improvement.
- Being able to identify the early stages of team dysfunction and taking corrective actions.
- Facilitating the development of reports for career development opportunities.

The additional points when managing remotely are:

- Having technical proficiency with all virtual communication vehicles.
- Being able to facilitate meetings on a face-to-face, online, video or audio basis, with an emphasis on being able to set a positive tone through electronic communication.
- Being able to coach, manage performance and give feedback, or mentor remotely.
- Being confident working across boundaries, acknowledging and optimising cultural differences.

- **Understanding and facilitating virtual team stages and dynamics.**
- **Being able to spend 70–80 per cent of time with the team who are *not* co-located with you.**
- **Managing projects and programmes, spreading the workload fairly, and avoiding over-committing members of the team.**

Getting the foundation stones right to make the team work

Many of the characteristics of a virtual team replicate normal team interaction. For example, all teams need to have a sense of purpose, whether they are virtual or otherwise. In a virtual team where you do not have the advantage of face-to-face meetings, there needs to be more regular and explicit checks about their purpose.

As a leader you need to gain the team members' commitment and make sure they understand the benefit both to themselves and to others from existing as a team. So why are they doing what they are doing? What would happen if we did not exist? If you asked someone in your team, 'What is your job?' and they just give a job title, you know that you have failed. Their answer should have been: 'I deliver x service (benefit), to internal/external customers.' Define early on team members' roles and responsibilities to minimise confusion, frustration and conflicts of interest.

In everyday life the one thing that people judge others from is their behaviour. It is your role to clarify acceptable modes of behaviour, which very much ties into the culture you are aiming to create, and ensure that all of you are working in the same direction. Don't allow misunderstandings to raise their head due to inappropriate behaviour.

The building of trust is critical given the absence of face-to-face contact. Trust takes on a whole new meaning in geographically distributed teams, and is measured almost exclusively in terms of reliability. For the leader, trust is expressed through consistency of purpose, and in his or her dealings with colleagues and others.

During any project or assignment there could be interim team members who join for a specific period of time to help the team realise its objectives. These could be either internal or external members. This is where your facilitation role kicks in. It is up to you to make sure they feel welcome, integrated and fully au fait with the technology available for their use, plus the processes and procedures that are in place for the project. Although new members can stimulate a virtual team, they may have problems figuring out how to enter a fast-moving discussion. You need to devise a way for people to enter or re-enter the team in midstream so that they are not only up to speed with pertinent information, but also have a team principle that others empathise with a new entrant to a discussion, and help them into the conversation.

A facilitation style of management works well in this instance, but when it comes to creating job descriptions, policy and procedures you need to adopt an authoritative style of leadership. Why is this? When people work in the same office together you can have loose job descriptions, possibly with two sharing elements of the same role. When working remotely there needs to be formalisation and accountability to avoid misunderstanding and chaos.

Policies and procedures

So, transparency and clear, agreed policies and procedures are vital. A well-managed virtual team is more of a hierarchy than a well-managed classic team.

As with any project, whether face-to-face or virtual, you should schedule in progress reviews and set milestones. In a virtual environment you need to be doubly vigilant as you do not have the advantage of corridor meetings or informal conversations with colleagues. Prior to the due date for an activity, send a reminder e-mail or voice message to those working remotely to ensure deadlines are going to be adhered to.

One of the issues you are going to face during the running of a project is to ensure that there is clarity about the decision-making process. If you are accustomed to working internationally you will be very aware that decision making might be deeply rooted in the various cultures you encounter around the world. For example, in Japan teams make decisions through a lengthy consensus process. A person wanting to make a proposal will talk informally to all possible people affected, and maybe send around a proposal to be approved by all the different teams concerned. A meeting might then be called, but it will be a rubber-stamping exercise in order to report back or to draw up action points. In the UK and United States, managers are taught to brainstorm information with their team, choose a direction quickly and make adjustments as the project moves forward. In France, the education system teaches that debate and confrontation are necessary parts of any decision-making process.

As the leader of the team you need to balance and weigh up all these different approaches, and clarify which approach should be adopted at different stages of a project. It will be challenging, but an explicit description of how a decision is to be made is critical to move a project forward internationally.

Communication

Ask the team what form of technology would help the team work well together. Technology can sometimes mean that technical assistance is required. Consider whether there is someone already in the team who can act as an informal helpdesk, or whether you need to find this facility outside the team.

In a virtual team people have the added responsibility for how they communicate with each other. There needs to be mutual agreement between parties as to what form of communication works best for each of them in various given situations. This needs to be explicit right from the word go.

Provide guidelines on how often to communicate and suggest regular frequency to create predictability, which will reduce the uncertainty of the team's coordination. For example, in one of the virtual teams that I was involved with we had a weekly Monday morning conference call to check the status and jointly work through any issues that might have arisen during the week. This worked well as we were all based in Europe, but this would not have been achievable if some of us were working in, for example, South East Asia or Australia. So, there needs to be respect and negotiation between all parties concerned with regard to the availability of members of the team who might be working in different time zones.

One of your options could be to set up a group forum via LinkedIn that is just for your team. This open forum is a place where anything can go; people in the team can bring up ideas for discussion, with the ground rule that comments and exchanges that follow need to be constructive, to ensure that all parties work positively together.

Few virtual teams are 100 per cent virtual. For the start of a project, if possible get the team members to meet on a face-to-face basis to establish relationships and clarify how they would like to link together given the project brief. This is particularly important for those who are interdependent.

You need to bear in mind that those working virtually don't have the benefit of going into a colleague's office to get advice, or to chat through a problem they are struggling with. The use of instant messaging, chat rooms or e-mail can help overcome this issue. In addition, social media such as wikis, blogs and social networks have created a virtual environment that more closely mimics the 'hallway' conversations and face-to-face meetings that used to take place when everything and everyone was located under one roof.

You should develop a simple approach to communicating urgent information, and 'Just-in-Time' information when it is required, and letting everyone take action in an independent fashion. Of course this means that those taking the information have to have sufficient intelligence, have received adequate training, and have background knowledge to know what to do with it. It puts the onus on you as the team leader to create an enabled/empowered environment, so that people in your virtual team realise they will receive information from you, not orders. This means developing autonomy and self-management wherever you can within the team.

In today's environment, speed is of essence. The one thing you don't want is for everything to stop when someone does not reply or is away from his or her screen, or a person's e-mail gets bounced. You must establish a code of conduct to avoid delays. For example, if there is a request for information, the recipient has to acknowledge the request within 24 or 48 hours, and if they can't deal with the request immediately they should flag when they can come back with a response. All parties then know where they stand.

When it relates to a common workload, your technology needs to log all actions, when they were taken, and by whom. This form of logging takes a degree of discipline as well. Over the years I have worked in different consultancy groups where a number of us have been dealing with the same client, and logged what we have done on the client's electronic record. On some occasions you come across 'lm4c' (ie left message for client), and a person's initials, and you have little or no idea whether you are supposed to be aware of this contact or not should you want to contact the client yourself. On other occasions consultants leave an essay! There clearly has to be a happy medium with client record information, and you should agree and set a common standard with your team.

To encourage productive conversations between members of the team, it is important that you create some kind of common cognitive ground for the group. Even teams from the same organisation who work regularly together can have a hard time developing conversations deep enough to be significant without there being some form of context framework to start off with. You could, for example, bring in someone who has worked on a similar project in the past to share their thoughts and findings in order to instigate ideas and a thought process in your team, or run a training session, or suggest a 'best practice' benchmarking visit locally for part of the team, who then feed back to the rest of the group. Any of these approaches could get the ball rolling.

Tips: How to communicate during videoconferencing

- **If English is your mother tongue, be wary that witty asides and sentences that tail off might not be understood by non-English speaking personnel.**
- **Use 'international' English – clear, short sentences, with a lot of clarifying and comprehensive checking statements and questions.**
- **If possible base your conversation on an agreed agenda, and use visual diagrams and illustrations to compound the message.**
- **Don't let your eyes wander around too much as if you are not listening or concentrating on the conversation in hand.**
- **Remember 'high context' cultures such as Japan prefer non-verbal clues such as body language, silences and voice tone; people from 'low context' cultures such as the United States, Germany and Australia prefer explicit verbal communication.**

As with any learning process in a 'normal' team, it is your role to facilitate and push boundaries. Get people to challenge an approach and come up with their own ideas for implementation. Through opening up discussion in the group, people are forced to dig deeper in their thought process, so that you can arrive at a consensus as to how you should progress.

Encourage openness between all members of the team. If there is poor communication between a couple of the members, encourage them to be open and frank as to why this is so and what can be done to improve the situation.

How about communication for coaching or mentoring processes? Skype has enabled not only one-to-one face-to-face contact for these processes, but also group video calling, which can help you coach several people at the same time.

CASE STUDY   Netmums, a parenting website

Siobhan Freegard, co-founder of the Netmums website, believes that knowing something about your work colleagues' personal life, not just work contact, can forge a stronger relationship between colleagues working virtually.

The 66 employees who work remotely meet regularly in 'the Pub', their online chat room dedicated to non-work matters. People might put up pictures of their children, or even discuss interpersonal problems they are having with their partner. They also have their Christmas party online, where everyone has their own bottle of wine on their desk!

(Chynoweth, 2010)

Information flow

When working on a project, people need to know how their part of the assignment fits into the bigger picture so they can make informed judgements. Project management schedule charts can be published on the internet using the team's website.

People's working hours, holiday leave, or business travel should, if possible, also be logged on an electronic calendar that is accessible to all. Business trips and travel can change by the day of course, so if a calendar is not that practical, ground rules could be established that if a team member is going to be out of town others in the team would be notified by telephone or e-mail.

The pace at which information flows has to be timely for everyone. You are aiming for a 'rolling present'. If there are various parts of the virtual team working in different time zones, you might need to slow the pace accordingly for all key decisions to make sure you are getting input from all parties concerned prior to moving forward. As the facilitator, if things are going slowly, communicate this. Remember, no news is still news. You can explain the rationale if relevant.

At the end of any assignment, tacit knowledge based on valuable experience should supplement the quantifiable data, giving your 'learning organisation' a complete management communications and decision-making process.

CASE STUDY   British Telecom's experience using virtual teams

British Telecom (BT) has found that allowing members of virtual teams to work from home has resulted in increased productivity and lower staff turnover rates.

In parts of the business there has also been a need to provide around the clock service. BT has developed a 'follow the sun' model of work that allows two engineering-maintenance teams, one based in Wales and the other in California, to share work virtually so they can provide 24/7 backup. To start off with it was a temptation for each team to blame the other if something went wrong. But over time this defensive attitude has reduced, and accountability has been instilled in the teams.

Creating trust and a sense of camaraderie

For a virtual team to work together successfully there are two vital ingredients. First, there needs to be mutual trust, in other words a shared belief that you can depend on each other to achieve a common purpose. Secondly, members of the team will want to have a sense of belonging, that they are part of a bigger whole, that they know more about their colleagues than just a telephone extension number and can call on them for help or advice if necessary. As the team leader you are the one to make this happen.

Let's start with a sense of belonging. Peter Drucker, the management guru, states:

> the leaders who work most effectively, it seems to me, never say 'I'. And that is not because they have trained themselves not to say 'I'. They don't think 'I'. They think 'we', they think 'team'. They understand their job to be to make the team function. They accept the responsibility and don't sidestep it, but 'we' get the credit. This is what creates trust, what enables you to get the task done. (Drucker, 2007)

You need to trust people unless you have good reason not to. When you trust people their self-respect grows and they will not want to let you down. If you treat them with suspicion, they will resent it, lose confidence in their own ability and then probably let you down.

Trust is also built through delegating wisely. Delegate the task, not the method. Make sure people know what is needed and, importantly, that they have the right skills, tools and resources to undertake the task in hand. Don't blame others if you delegate badly.

Drive out fear in your virtual working environment. Remember that people you don't see on a regular basis may be more reticent about flagging problem areas and issues that concern them. Value criticism – use it to improve products, processes and procedures. Above all else, don't shoot the messenger! Discuss all aspects of organisational life – nothing should be off-limits. Practise collaborative decision making, and challenge worst-case thinking by also exploring the upside and build action plans for all cases, including contingency arrangements.

Tips: How to create trust and camaraderie in a virtual team

- Make sure that all members of the team feel they have fair access to you as their leader. Don't just favour those that are located at the same site as you.
- Show consistency in your behaviour – this relates to your reliability and predictability. It also determines your ability and good judgement in handling situations.
- Overtly show loyalty and demonstrate integrity to your team. You can do this by protecting others and being on the same side, both when they are present and, most importantly, in their absence.
- People need to know more about the colleagues they are working with, not just about the task in hand. A group chat room can act as a coffee dispenser/water cooler where people meet to chat about their everyday lives, swap stories about their weekend or holidays they have taken.
- Keep your written communication in a positive forward-looking mode. If you need to take corrective action with regard to performance, or because of interpersonal conflict, choose another mode of communication – face-to-face meetings/Skype/ telephone, conference calls, etc.
- From the word go, schedule virtual meetings with your team in your calendar.
- Your capacity to listen is key to the exchanges you have in a virtual environment. You don't have the

advantage of being able to read body language, or hear the casual concern that someone might voice to you passing in the corridor. Actively listen, probe and question that bit more than you would working in a face-to-face environment.

- Members of the team need to have clear guidelines on where to go for information or resources. They should have easy ways to be introduced to each other, not having to access everything and everyone through you as the team leader.
- Include measuring people on their teamwork and sharing of information in their performance review.
- Make sure that recognition and reward are fairly distributed to all members of your team, not just those that are closest to hand. (Recognition and reward can be as simple as 'Good work' or, 'I can see you went the extra mile to put this proposal together' – it's not just about financial reward.)
- In an interpersonal conflict situation aim to be objective and show fairness to all parties concerned. Once again, do not show favouritism to those who work at the same site as you do.

Tackling problems in virtual teams

Technology has enabled independent players to be no longer isolated, and teams to be created by staff based around the world. This is the good news. The bad news is that there are certain problems that can arise, which could easily be nipped in the bud if team members are all based in one location, but prove to be more challenging when staff are working remotely. Staff are two and a half times more likely to experience teamwork problems with distant colleagues, and issues are harder to solve.

What are some of the common problems that might occur, and the danger signs to look out for? Let's start with the danger signs:

- **unsatisfactory reporting process, or communication of status updates;**
- **a wall of silence between co-workers: phone calls being screened or not being returned, e-mails not being answered, or key decisions being made without consultation with co-workers;**
- **burn out – morale being at rock bottom.**

This can end up with:

- **people asking to be relocated to another project, or a project leader asking for someone to be removed from the team;**
- **an increase in customer complaints;**
- **loss of business.**

Problems such as these can occur for a myriad of reasons. If you are the manager of a large team spread around the world with local managers reporting into you, avoid the temptation to micromanage the situation – trying to tackle the individual or team problem yourself rather than working jointly with the local manager. The local manager has to have the authority and wherewithal to take things forward him or herself. Coach or advise this person by all means, but don't take away his or her authority and self-esteem.

With a smaller team that directly reports into you, as has been mentioned previously, invest time upfront in setting the ground rules and defining expectations with regard to behaviour, timeliness and communication methodology. *The critical factor with this is to get each person in the team to agree to these standards.* Should problems subsequently occur, call a meeting but don't discuss the specific content of individual concerns or past problems; instead, reset expectations that everyone can agree to going forward.

If you need to hold a member of the team accountable for his or her actions, such as violating agreed ground rules, do so on a one-to-one basis, not in a public arena. This should ideally be done face-to-face, and if this is not possible, use one of the communication methods that we have looked at already in this chapter. Use anything but e-mail. There needs to be an exchange between both parties, not a written dump of complaints.

As part of the culture you have set, encourage staff to talk candidly and openly to each other, always keeping in mind that those they are talking to might have an inborn resistance to communicating in this manner. Education and cultural considerations can have a lasting hold on how a person interacts in the business world.

In the virtual world there needs to be more vigilant activity in getting feedback from your clients. What went well/where is there room for improvement? Celebrate your clients' success, put them on your website, in your newsletter or company magazine.

The virtual world of the future – the rise of the neo-nomad

In an increasingly virtual world, the old way of arranging work around companies, countries and regions will break down. I believe that rather than cut-throat competition, be it between individuals, departments, or companies, tomorrow's business processes and innovation will be defined by collaboration.

Companies will put together people from different nationalities, cultures, backgrounds and specialisms to enhance creativity and innovation. Virtual innovation centres exist already, which allow companies to ask, 'We have a problem, does anyone want to solve it?' This can mean that a group can be formed with members coming from anywhere in the world, who can put themselves forward to solve the problem that has been raised.

In 2005, groups of website developers, programmers and entrepreneurs moved around remotely in the Bay Area just north of Silicon Valley in the United States and became known as the 'neo-nomad's or 'digital Bedouins'. They were known by this name because of their use of technology and the latest generation of web-based tools. Another nickname was the 'Starbucks society', as they used the coffee shop location with its good Wi-Fi facilities. Working in consultancy groups over the years I have found that I and work colleagues were nomads as we travelled the world forming different groups as the various assignments required. The lifestyle has been nomadic, and e-mail has obviously been a good method of us all linking together, but Wi-Fi has not always been as accessible as we would have wished. In the United States and Canada, Wi-Fi access has been commonplace, but in Western Europe it is at best patchy, especially outside the major commercial centres. The problem currently is there are many incompatible Wi-Fi providers and often you need to subscribe to a number of various services.

All of this is gradually changing though, with GPRS and 3G networks offering 'anytime/anyplace' access in quite remote places. WiMax looks as if it may be a promising alternative to other forms of broadband, as does the recently investigated idea of direct satellite access without having to route the signal through terrestrial stations. This will mean that a nomadic professional lifestyle will be far more achievable for those with specialist knowledge who do not need to be located in one particular place such as a company office. They can collaborate with others who have similar or complementary skills, and market themselves to multiple organisations and work on several different projects at the same time.

Finally: technology and the virtual working world have proven to be both a blessing and a curse. On one hand they have reduced the tyranny of distance and isolation, but on the other hand they have created the possibility of new communication barriers – avoidance of tackling issues head on, lack of ownership – 'That's a head office decision, don't blame me' – and put new people-management demands on those heading up the team.

Teleworking and virtual teams are not only here to stay, but are becoming the new business model for organisations' survival in this ever-competitive global economy.

Checklist for action

- If you are leading a virtual team, provide clearly defined direction and remove all ambiguity from the process. Policies and procedures need to be clearly defined, and behavioural interaction instilled from the word go. The style of management you adopt should be authoritative to start off with, and then facilitative when the timing feels right.
- Are you spending the appropriate mix of time (ideally 70–80 per cent) with those who are not co-located with you? If not, redress the balance.
- Ensure that the decision-making process you use for the next international assignment is clearly defined and understood by all parties concerned. Take into account the fact that cultural approaches will differ, and decide and define to all in the team which approach should be used, when, during the assignment.
- Review the flow of information to ensure all are aware of the bigger picture, and aim for a 'rolling present'.
- Take a new look at the workload of your team to see where else you might be able to outsource a service or facility with a view to building competitive advantage.

9

The future for teams

As we have seen throughout the book, change and restructuring is a given. Teams are popular because they work and businesses are operating with fewer staff than ever before. Fewer people are doing more work, and there are fewer layers in the (lean) organisation. Skills such as coordination, planning, recruitment, performance and quality management are no longer the domain of managers alone. These responsibilities are increasingly becoming the responsibility of the team. In turn, as teams move from being leader-led to self-managed, responsibilities are being shifted from individual accountability to collective mutual (team) accountability. At the same time, there will always be a requirement for traditional work groups formed around common technical or functional skills and areas of expertise – for example accounting, production or HR.

I predict that virtual teams will be increasingly prevalent as organisations capitalise on globalisation. Trade barriers are falling, and growth of new markets, such as China, Brazil and India, is now the norm. Multicultural teams will rule the day. Organisational culture dominated by Head Office (HO) will no longer work. The rule will be guidelines in the form of vision, strategies, values and competencies from HO that are adapted by local teams to best fit with local cultural and 'social need' circumstances. We live in an interdependent world economy. New middle classes are emerging around the world with consumer spend reflecting this development and rising resource prices impacting us all.

As a manager you must be aware of how far you can adapt and adopt local values, behaviours and language to the required organisational values, behaviours and language set by HO, and ensure you commit to the 'social needs' of your team members so that they feel valued as a member of the team and that the team as a whole delivers tangible value back to the organisation and its stakeholders. This will become more crucial as teams become even more fluid with members reporting into several managers, which in turn will have an impact on how performance will be evaluated and reward and compensation packages be developed to reflect this new reality.

Management is a challenge. It's also very stimulating and exciting. Tomorrow's managers will need real 'social' skills to make team members' roles in the team rewarding and meaningful. Relationships with team members will more often take place online or over Skype. Managers will have to be accessible and open to team members' requests rather than orchestrating centralised controls.

> Team leadership is much more an art, a belief, a condition of the heart than a set of things to do. (DePree, 1990)

References and recommended reading

Atkinson, W (2008) Novellus realises benefits of early supplier involvement, *Purchasing*, 10 April

Belasco, J A and Stayer, R C (1994) *Flight of the Buffalo: Soaring to excellence. Learning to let employees lead*, Warner Books, New York

Belbin, R M (2003) *Team Roles at Work*, Butterworth-Heinemann, Oxford

Biafore, B (2006) *On Time! On Track! On Target!*, Microsoft Press, Birmingham

Buzan, T (2010) *Use Your Head: How to unleash the power of your mind*, BBC Books, London

Chynoweth, C (2010) Is there anyone out there? Bosses of virtual teams need to make time to keep everyone in the loop, *The Sunday Times*, 25 July

Clark, L (2008) Swatches: keep the brand new, *The Statesman* (India), 16 March

Colenso, M (2000) *Kaizen Strategies for Improving Team Performance*, Pearson Education, Harlow de Bono, E (1999) *Six Thinking Hats: An essential approach to business management*, Back Bay Books, New York

DePree, M (1990) *Leadership is an Art*, Bantam Doubleday Dell, New York

Drucker, P (2007) *Management Challenges for the 21st Century*, 2nd revd edn, Butterworth-Heinemann, Oxford

Fisher, K (2000) *Leading Self-directed Work Teams: A Guide to developing new team leadership skills*, McGraw-Hill, New York

Gale, S F (2000) The little airplane that could, *Training*, December, pp 60–67

Goleman, D (1996) *Emotional Intelligence and Working with Emotional Intelligence*, Bloomsbury Publishing, London

Handy, C (1995) Trust and the virtual organization, *Harvard Business Review*

Hazrati ,V (2010) *Most Effective Team Structure*, www.infoq.com/news/2010/03/most-effective-team-structure, 16 March

Heath, N (2010) Severn Trent on how virtualisation is taking the pain out of the office move, *SILCOM*, 8 October

Henry, S M and Stevens, K T (1999) Using Belbin's leadership role to improve team effectiveness: an empirical investigation, *Journal of Systems and Software*, **44** (3), pp 241–50

Katzenbach, J R and Smith, D K (2003) *The Wisdom of Teams*, Harper Business Essentials, London

Kerzner, H (2003) *Project Management Workbook*, Wiley, New York

Kotter, J (1990) *A Force for Change*, Free Press, New York

Kotter, J (2010) *Leading Change: Why transformational efforts fail*, Harvard Business School Publishing, Boston, MA

McCormack, M (1984) *What They Don't Teach You at Harvard Business School*, Bantam Books, New York

Maslow, H (1943) A theory of human motivation, *Psychological Review*, **50** (4), pp 370–96

Micklethwait, J and Woolridge, A (1997) *The Witch Doctors*, Mandarin Paperbacks, London

Norris, S (2007) Cooperatives pay big dividends, *The Guardian*, 30 March

Osborn, A (1953) *Applied Imagination*, Charles Scribner, New York

Parnes, S J, Noller, R B and Biondi, A M (1977) *Guide to Creative Action*, Charles Scribner, New York

Revans, R (1980) *Action Learning: New techniques for management*, Blond & Briggs, London

Robbins, H and Finley, M (2000) *Why Teams Don't Work*, Time Warner, New York

Tamkin, P, Pearson, G, Hirsh, W and Constable, S (2010) Exceeding expectation: The principles of outstanding leadship, The Work Foundation

Tuckman, B W (1965) Developmental sequences in small groups, *Psychological Bulletin*, **66** (6), pp 384–99

Wellington, P (1995) *Kaizen Strategies for Customer Care*, FT Prentice Hall, Harlow

Yalom, I D (1970) *The Theory and Practice of Group Psychotherapy*, New York, Basic Books